NOW BUILD AND RUN A PROFITABLE MICROLENDING BUSINESS

The sustainable microfinance

A concise guide

Dr Norman A. Naaman

PREFACE

Micro-Finance Institutions (MFIs) play a crucial role in elevating the living standards of low-income communities through financial inclusion by enabling access to capital especially for small and micro businesses. Because of the negative disparities between the number of college graduates churned out annually from institutions of higher learning and the number of blue-collar jobs created annually, entrepreneurship has now become a veritable alternative for many young people in the world today. To continue playing their assumed role of financial inclusion, MFIs must ensure their sustainability through sustainable financial performance proof. The book takes cognizant of the fact that MFIs have double –bottom-line objectives. First is financial inclusion and therefore poverty reduction and, second, financial sustainability.

Barter trade must have been a real act of faith then. No standard medium of exchange. The evolution into a money system has definitely expanded trade and tremendously raised the comfort levels of the whole human race. Absence of financial services including deposit accounts, savings plans, debit cards, credit cards, mobile money etc. means unimaginable life without financial services and yet there's still a significant portion of humans still financially excluded. In fact, recent data has shown nearly half of the global population still endures life without financial services. Reliance on age-old informal mechanisms is still prevalent. These mechanisms are quite expensive and involve such exercises as livestock keeping as a form of savings, village/extended family altruistic feasts as an insurance scheme against unforeseen adversities.

Current research demonstrates that appropriate financial services can lead to higher household welfare as well as spur enterprise activity. At a macro level, it has been proved that economies with high rates of financial inclusion report faster growth rates than those with high financial exclusion rates.

The Sustainable Microfinance book reflects the current opportunities existing in the market for those who would like to make a contribution to societal economic development while at the same time ensuring an attractive economic return to themselves. It recognizes the gap in knowledge that exists on what it entails to operate a profitable and responsible microfinance business in addition to defining its objectives. With a better understanding of what it is, what it does, how it is done together with how innovations in financial products can be leveraged, it is my belief that a lot more people with the will, desire and means will venture into microfinance and see financial exclusion eradicated and contribute to the nation good of improved living standards, freedom from servitude and broader participation in the governance of national resources. We have the Capital (either intellectual including learned skills or money) to raise people from poverty.

DEDICATION

This book is dedicated to the many workers who daily wake up worried of the sustainability of their current jobs! Freedom to choose, to be a person, to be emancipated, to be freed from servitude.

You have options. Just dare to look.

Chapter 1 Table of Contents

PREFACE   II

DEDICATION   III

CHAPTER 2 INTRODUCTION   - 1 -

   Background - 1 -
   Why this Book   - 3 -

CHAPTER 3 MICROFINANCE BASICS   - 4 -

   Defining the Microfinance Concept   - 4 -
   Double Bottom-lines in Microfinance Concept   - 4 -
   The Meaning of Sustainability - 5 -
   Microfinance Financial Sustainability   - 6 -
   Subsidy and Sustainability   - 6 -
   MFIs Capital Structure Impact on Sustainability   - 7 -
   MFI Efficiency   - 7 -

CHAPTER 4 THE MICRO FINANCE INDUSTRY - 8 -

   Introduction - 8 -
   Sector Size and Outreach   - 9 -
   Sector Strategy and Prospects - 12 -
   Product Innovation and Focus / Specialisation   - 13 -
   Operational efficiency and Technology Leverage - 13 -
   Credit Processes and Analytics   - 14 -

CHAPTER 5 FINANCIAL ACCESS IN KENYA   - 16 -

   Financial health and inclusion - 16 -
   Demographics   - 17 -
   Occupation and Consumption Patterns - 17 -
   Dealing with Disturbances/Emergencies   - 19 -
   Usage of Financial Services   - 20 -

Application of Credit - 20 -
Access to Financial Channels & Providers   - 21 -

CHAPTER 6 OPERATING A MICROFINANCE BUSINESS   - 22 -

Funding your micro-lending business   - 22 -
Introduction - 22 -
Grants and soft credit from donors and governments   - 23 -
Client Savings accounts   - 23 -
Private Sector funding (Private equity) - 23 -
Equity (Owner Capital)   - 24 -
The microfinance funding stages   - 24 -
Source: hdl.handle.net   - 25 -
Funding Mechanisms Innovation   - 25 -
Credit Guarantees   - 25 -
Securitization   - 26 -
Specialized equity funds   - 26 -
Capital Raising Strategies   - 26 -
Establishing a microfinance business   - 27 -
The need for research   - 27 -
Client profiling   - 27 -
Regulatory Framework   - 28 -
Processes   - 28 -
Competition - 28 -
Management Information Systems   - 29 -
Technology - 29 -
Network   - 29 -
Agent network   - 29 -
Business model selection   - 30 -
Products and Services   - 30 -
Loan products   - 31 -
Savings schemes   - 32 -
Insurance services   - 32 -

  Integrative approaches   *- 33 -*
  Your microfinance business' success   *- 33 -*
  Credit Underwriting Models   *- 34 -*
  Loan Collection models   *- 34 -*
  Conclusion   *- 48 -*

CHAPTER 7 MICROFINANCE PERFORMANCE MONITORING   - 49 -

  CREDIT ANALYSES ....- 56 -
  LOAN COLLECTION RATES ....- 56 -
  FINANCIAL ANALYSES ....- 57 -

Chapter 2 INTRODUCTION

Background

Microfinance Institutions (MFIs) typically target providing financing solutions to the low-income sector of the population in the regions they operate in. It is sometimes assumed that microfinance and micro credit is one and the same thing. The difference is that microfinance goes beyond credit and includes other services akin to banking and insurance like micro-savings and bancassurance geared towards serving the lower end of the economy while operating in varied forms, from non-governmental organizations, non-deposit taking/credit only operators, deposit taking operators, to Credit Unions/savings and cooperative societies (Saccos) etc. MFIs have been reported to price for the high risks inherent in the sector they target and thus typically charge more for their services relative to the commercial/retail banks. They also exhibit short-term structures in their lending profiles, but their lending practices are less collateralized as compared to banks. Research, such as published on www.microfinancegateway.org, has shown that MFIs have enabled a lot of entrepreneurs who don't own assets for collateral to *'escape positions as poorly paid wage laborers or farmers……………. have expanded the frontiers of institutional finance and have brought the poor, especially poor women, into the formal financial system by enabling them to access credit in order to fight poverty.'*

There have been signs that MFIs could be effective at fighting poverty through their easy ways of providing credit unlike banks that require onerous document submission that only formal businesses and salaried individuals can provide. For instance, banks will usually need a business to have been profitable for a minimum 3-year period with audited financial statements which the informal sector does not have. Even where the documentation is availed, the last disappointment is usually the provision of collateral. This has ensured that the poor-uneducated are excluded from credit and hence unable to scale their small ventures up leave alone to start up. Professor Mohamed Yunus' Grameen bank model continues to be replicated across the globe as a response to ensuring financial inclusion of the poor.

In spite of the proliferation of MFIs, including the unregulated ones, large sections of poor neighbourhoods in the developing economies are still excluded. This is the result, mainly, of the commercialization of these MFIs thus creating a supply-side problem (outreach inadequacy). This outreach inadequacy emanates from the constraints of costs of sustaining operations as well as capital sources. It is noteworthy to remember that in spite of the unmet demand, MFIs will still need to address the moral hazard and adverse selection problems in the sector as capital becomes available to them in order to remain financially sustainable.

Hitherto, there's still a large portion of the poor who can't access finance in the developing countries, more so, in Africa. The existing MFIs face inefficiency and capital challenges that have prevented them from meeting the demand for microfinance services in these economies. Additionally, the high lending interest rates could be a barrier to many low-income communities that need to access finance as it has been shown that credit demand among the financially excluded is not necessarily inelastic. That is, the uptake of credit has a limit depending on the price charged and other conditions.

A number of authors have argued that institutionists raise up the notion of competition through the forces of supply and demand and therefore Adam Smith's invisible hand which stabilizes prices as the solution to the financial sustainability and outreach challenges of MFIs. This, of course, implies that competition will weed out unsustainable MFIs and ensure the blooming and expansion of the competitive better run ones. And, in the end the winners will introduce altruistic (living for the sake of others) behavior and share the surplus with the poor through expanded outreach. Such an expectation has never been met where the pursuit of profit is the primary objective. However, the commercialization proposition has led to a mushrooming of microcredit organizations with a lot of not-for-profit organizations converting into formalized retail banks with an eclectic supply of a product shelf. This has been made possible with private equity firms providing the capital and management addition. This therefore puts pressure on the people who run the MFIs to deliver efficiency and sustainable returns.

It is important to underscore the fact that MFI financial sustainability lays at the core of institutional sustainability in fighting poverty and thus possible collapses of MFIs due to financial unsustainability will harm the poor most. There are a lot of documented arguments for better not having MFIs than operating unsustainable ones and thus one the reason of writing this simple book is to lay out a simple blueprint for establishing, building, and running a profitable and sustainable microfinance outfit business.

There are currently coordinated policy responses from governmental institutions and donor bodies to promote competition among moneylenders as well as measures to ensure financial sustainability in lending institutions to enhance the breadth of credit outreach (thus expand the credit access in a responsible manner). This book is a simple guide on how to establish, build and run a sustainable microfinance business for those who wish to directly participate in reaching the lower end of the economic spectrum and still have far reaching economic returns to themselves.

Why this Book

The role of MFIs in uplifting the economic communities has been underscored in the financial literature. It is now a given that MFIs are expected to continue playing this role of availing responsible finance to the financially excluded groups. For MFIs to play this role sustainably as going concerns, they need to demonstrate ability to continually generate revenues exceeding their costs. This sustainable profitability trend ensures that an MFI is able to attract the requisite additional funding for onward lending to the targeted groups. This book considers the clients and their needs whether they know them or are ignorant of them and how the suppliers of micro-financial services can meet these needs. The result, hopeful, is a how to book rather than a description of what! The book will therefore answer the following questions:

　　i.　　What is the purpose of microfinance?
　　ii.　　What are the demographic considerations involved in microfinance product innovation and offering?
　　iii.　　What ensures MFI Sustainability (financial and operational)?

Chapter 3 MICROFINANCE BASICS

Defining the Microfinance Concept

Different scholars and organizations define microfinance institutions differently only converging on the essence/function(s). To some, microfinance is defined in relation to the scale of financial services provision as well as to the target up takers. Thus, microfinance relates to small or limited financial services provision and is set up for the low income or unbanked segment of the population.

Others contend that the scope of services provision is broad and includes loans, deposits (savings options), transactions services including payments, money transfers just as conventional banking only that the target market is the poor and low-income households including farm and non-farm based micro-businesses.

However, it is important to take cognizance of the fact that there exist MFIs that provide social intermediation services like formation of groups, self-confidence development, financial literacy coaching, and management skills building to the targeted groups particularly low-income communities beyond financial intermediation. This is premised on the understanding that finance in itself is ineffective in poverty alleviation if not backed up by skills and person development support.

As Ledgerwood (2012) puts it: *"microfinance approach is not a minimalist approach offering only financial intermediation but an integrated approach offering both financial intermediation and the other services mentioned."*

From the foregoing, we understand that Microfinance institutions act as social and economic emancipation tools and are effective complements of the conventional banking sector with special attention to the poor. The rationale of the financial inclusion for the poor is justifiable on the basis that the empowerment of the poor through the creation of income generation capacities opens access to development prerequisites and thus reduces vulnerabilities to unexpected occurrences.

Double Bottom-lines in Microfinance Concept

Microfinance Institutions face a constrained dual operational objective function that needs to be optimized. The two competing objectives centre around society and sustainability (continuing operations). These two performance objectives of financial sustainability and social sustainability place MFIs in a peculiar situation and any evaluation efforts on MFIs cannot prefer one to the other. There are arguments to the effect that the two functions operate independent of each other and thus can be pursued separately without affecting each other. This implies the pursuit of the profit motive that ensures financial sustainability but does nothing for the poor or financially excluded.

It is believed that MFIs are effective reversers of poverty trends where there's an entrepreneurial spirit. There are indications that MFIs had expanded their reach wild-wide to over 100 million people across the globe by the end of the last decade and the reach is expanding. The principal aim is reaching the unbanked while not losing sight of financial sustainability (a dual objective function). It is one thing to reach the unbanked and initiate a number of financial solutions and it is another to ensure that the MFI is available in future as demand rises either from scale opportunities of initial entrepreneurs or the mere growth in the number of poor neighbourhoods needing solutions. Hence, making profit is vitally important.

Best practice MFI assessment therefore follows the double-bottom-line template. The concern has been that the pursuit of profit might compromise the original mission of reaching the poor. Studies also suggest that a profit motivated MFI sector requires attention to efficiency and drive to develop and create new markets and credit products offering leading to better service to the poor.

The Meaning of Sustainability

Financial sustainability in MFIs could as well be the main overriding dimension in the whole spectrum of Sustainability of MFIs. Financial sustainability is the ability of an MFI to produce enough revenues from operations that can cover its operating costs and thus enable the MFI to grow towards self-reliance. This makes it possible for the MFI to operate without donor support and ultimately generate revenues that apart from just covering its costs also return a profit.

Financial sustainability is measured in two ways: operational sustainability with a return of positive net operating income before inclusion of finance costs and financial self-sufficiency with above zero earnings after interest. MFIs that return below zero earnings after finance costs are considered financially unsustainable. Research has shown that there is a negative relationship between subsidies and sustainability, implying that high subsidies signify a dependency ratio that makes financial sustainability of an MFI untenable. However, it has been established that a high equity component in the funding structure makes a firm more financially sustainable. Microanalyses have shown that profitability is a necessary condition for an MFIs ability to get external funding.

Microfinance Financial Sustainability

MFI financial sustainability is the principal dimension of microfinance sustainability. This dimension refers to an MFI's ability in covering all its costs from internally generated operational income without outside support. Thus, operational self-dependence is the essence of financial sustainability. This definition has undertones of surplus income (profit) potential that hedges an MFI against future operational underperformance. We thus propose a two-stage measurement of financial sustainability as: 1) operational sustainability and 2) financial self-sufficiency where operational sustainability ensures coverage of operational costs from business/operations income whether there exist subsidies or not. Financial self-sufficiency obtains when an MFI can take care of its operations' finance costs from its own generated cash as well as other support (subsidy) at market value. This leads the following conclusions:

> *An MFI in loss position (indicating poor performance) cannot be said to be financially sustainable. An MFI returning a profit (after covering part of its operating costs with subsidies) is also not financially sustainable.*

Subsidy and Sustainability

Because many MFI programs world over are subsidized in varied ways, the sustainability of these subsidies is of crucial interest. The common illustration of this point is exemplified by Grameen Bank of Bangladesh which though with high loan service rates, still had a high reliance on subsidies given its higher social impact value. Some studies have uncovered negative correlations between quarterly subsidies and financial sustainability, however, with falling financial sustainability as subsidy income rose. In spite of arguments for subsidies helping MFIs reach up to desired scale, subsidies seem to, at times, encourage the wrong behavior in MFI management. A negative correlation exists between dependency ratio (donated equity/total capital) and financial sustainability. A declining dependency ratio in the MFI sector over time indicates self-sustainability, profitability and self-sufficiency.

MFIs Capital Structure Impact on Sustainability

Profitability could be affected by the mix of the different capital sources and, hence, MFI sustainability. Loans, deposits of various types (savings, fixed, checking accounts) and owner contribution (shares) form the primary funding sources of MFIs.

Capital structure impact on financial sustainability studies have had mixed results. Some have found a positive relationship between leverage and MFI ability to deal with moral hazard and adverse selection problems. However, other research show that although capital structure affects financial sustainability, financial sustainability is not improved by mere different capital sources. Equity capital is preferred and improves financial sustainability, as it is a cheaper source. Thus, the source of an MFIs funding has a bearing on its sustainability and should be given preeminence before setting up an MFI.

MFI Efficiency

We define efficiency as *"the ability to produce maximum output at a given level of input, and it is the most effective way of delivering small loans to the very poor in microfinance context" (see* docplayer.net) This is achieved through operational optimization solutions (cost minimization and operating maximization) subject to budget constraints. Efficiency's impact on MFI financial self- sustainability has been argued to be enduring. This implies that it can be quantified by productivity measures such as the number of loans/staff as well as by cost management measures such as cost per loan. In this regard, studies on village banking financial viability argue that "the numbers of borrowers and the cost per borrower" are variables correlating highly with financial sustainability. Productivity is a significant variable determining profitability. A study carried out on a Tanzanian rural MFI established statistically significant negative relationship between number of borrowers per staff and financial sustainability. This was justified on the strength that rural MFI staff lacked efficiency and thus fail to manage borrowers as the numbers rise resulting in MFIs' unsustainability. Management inefficiency and portfolio at risk have been found to be detrimental to financial sustainability. Cost efficiency deteriorates with rising leverage implying an agency cost problem.

Chapter 4 THE MICRO FINANCE INDUSTRY

Introduction

The Association of Microfinance Institutions of Kenya (AMFI) has reported that the Kenyan microfinance sector ranks high among the Sub-Saharan countries in Africa as relates to vibrancy, diversity, and development state. The industry's diversity is observed its composition, which is made up of the corporate forms of deposit taking microfinance institutions, non-deposit taking (also known as credit only) micro-finance institutions (and otherwise appropriately better known as emergency lenders) as well as savings and credit cooperatives or Saccos (also called credit unions), most of which operate on a model of a fairly large distribution of brick and mortar branch network to reach and serve the financially excluded. The non-corporate type operators such as money lenders, digital lenders, Rotating Savings and Credit Associations (ROSCAs) (also called Mary-go-round groups and Accumulating Savings & Credit Associations (ASCAs) are also included in the description of the microfinance market.

The micro finance activities have been unregulated in Kenya over a long time, but this has now changed following the passage of the law that now brings all lenders under the Central Bank of Kenya regulation in 2022. Hitherto, the lack of regulation has enabled the continuous innovations and the ease of entry into and exit out of the sector. For instance, operations were set up with ease with no barriers such as the need to raise regulatory minimum capital and thus a mushrooming of microfinance operators in this environment. Another phenomenon of note is the market shift from dependence on poverty alleviation focused institutions that were donor funded and managed to for-profit organizations with a clear recognition from the public and governments that regulation of MFIs was necessary, especially for the credit-only institutions that looked forward to converting into deposit taking microfinance institutions and the 'digital' lenders where it was considered that their operations if not monitored, could easily be inconsiderate to the borrowers especially around pricing and collection methods/practices.

On the credit unions (or saccos) front, a new formal institutional type 'Deposit-taking SACCOs' has now been added to the current list of regulated institutions following the enacting of the deposit-taking SACCOs Act. These regulatory regulations have been in place since June 2011.

The industry delivers its offering to the market in the form of groups based lending, individual lending, corporate lending, and non-formal lending. The wide telecommunication network has had a bearing on the lending to the far-flung rural areas which are characterized by illiteracy, poor infrastructure and vicious cycle of poverty as described by the Association of Microfinance Institutions of Kenya (AMFI-Kenya). The thriving existence and expansion of the MFI players with the social and economic factors impact has transformed the industry to being viewed as an icon in the economy of Kenya hence the keen interest from the government and international investors in ensuring the MFI industry's responsible growth. Kenya's Vision 2030 includes and The Economic Pillar with the objective to improve and raise deposit mobilization levels by increasing savings to consumption ratios and improving the general quality of life for all citizens. To realise this vision, the government introduced regulatory laws through the Microfinance Act 2006 and continues to introduce amendments to ensure the industry is able to meet its objectives of serving the financially excluded.

Sector Size and Outreach

Portfolio Size.

The most recent data published by AMFI shows that the Gross Outstanding Portfolio in the industry stands at about Kshs 67 billion while the Portfolio at Risk above 30 days (PAR 30) had reached Kshs 7.8 billion. The total industry's number of loans peaked at 614,331 while the consolidated number of active clients had reached 2.1 million. Savers that were considered to be actively using the savings product were 1.6 million while those actively borrowing are approximately half a million.

Portfolio quality

The Industry's current non-performing loan portfolio is approximately 7.8 billion ranging between 1-day to 365-days and above 365-days. The following pie chart shows the percentages of how the portfolio at risk varied differently within the different days.

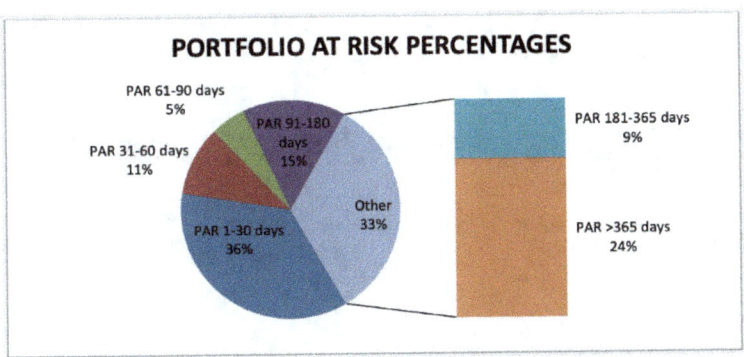

Source: AMFI 2021

Financial Structure, Solvency and Liquidity

The MFI sector is predominantly funded from client deposits. The credit only segment is funded via borrowed funds.

The total liabilities and equity of the sector amounted to 96.7 billion shillings where it was at its highest in the year 2016 and lowest in 2017 over the four years of 96.7 billion shilling 84% came from liabilities and 16% came from Equity. The industry shared the total liabilities as follows; Microfinance banks 59%, SACCO 29% and Credit Only Institutions 12%. Total assets amounted to 96.8 billion shillings.

In terms of market share, Microfinance banks accounts for 58.8%, Credit only 11.7% and he SACCO 29.5%. The chart below shows the asset size per year for the last 3 years (as at end of 2016).

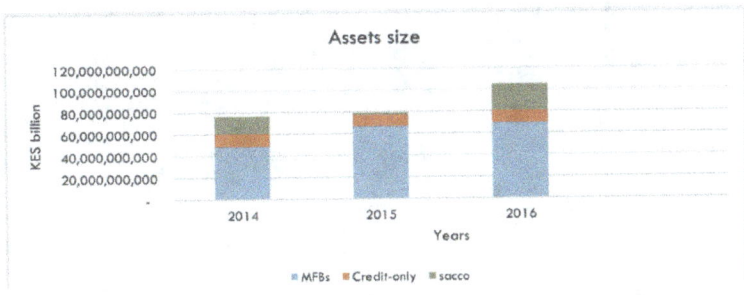

Profitability and Sustainability

The MFIs sector profitability and sustainability has remained high since 2016 with positive returns on equity and assets (ROE and ROA) and operational self-sufficiency (OSS).

	ROE	ROA	OSS
Credit-only MFIs	14.5%	3.3%	119%
MFBs	11.6%	1.5%	109%
Whole Sector without banks	12.8%	2.0%	112%

Source: AMFI 2017 Report

Credit Only Microfinance Industry Analysis

Loan Book Distribution

A larger part of the microfinance institutions (MFIs) assets are comprised of advances of business enterprise finance (57% of the lending). In sectoral terms, agriculture and consumption lending take up the next major buckets. The small, medium, and micro enterprises are the main MFI's niche segments when it comes to business finance. MFIs play in other segments remains low, presenting potential entrance opportunities.

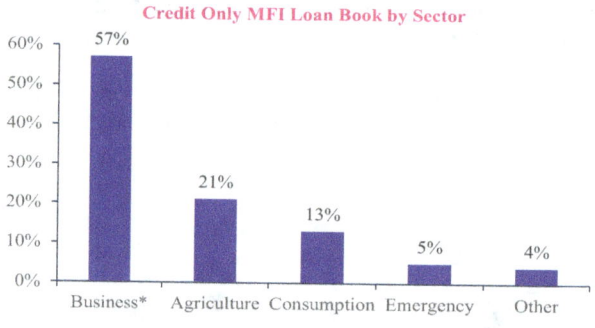

Source: realpeople.co.ke.   *Business enterprise financing

Top Credit Only MFIs in Kenya

The apex Credit Only MFIs in Kenya make up 82% of the sector earning assets, with the top 3 institutions being Real People, Platinum Credit and Greenland Fedha. These have posted positive asset growth in the recent past.

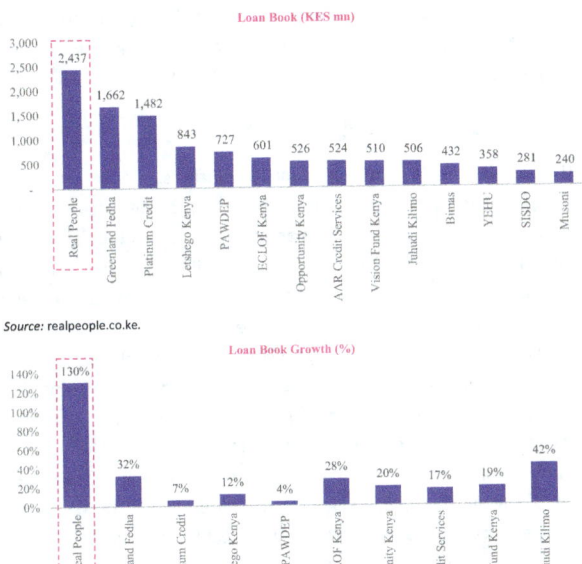

Source: realpeople.co.ke.

Sector Strategy and Prospects

The small business (micro and SME) market continues to make a significant contribution to Kenya's GDP expansion as well as job creation with annual rates of growths of between 8-10% out of the rapid urbanization that has led to an expanded goods and services demand due to an ever increasing customer base. The segment's perception of it being of high risk has meant that its access to finance is either costly or very limited. The MFI sector has survived by building a deeper understanding of the needs of its clients. The MFI sector has created and implemented ways and means to better assess and understand the micro and SME client affordability and willingness to pay, resulting in better risk management practices being deployed. It has also developed tools and practices of focus in ensuring a positive customer experience. This is achieved by providing convenience and a superior and compelling customer value proposition to the niche market segment.

Notwithstanding the ever rising scramble and competition in the microlending business, interested entrants can still craft growth strategies anchored and supported by the following initiatives and pillars:

Product Innovation and Focus / Specialisation

One of the growth approaches in the microlending business that enhances competitive positioning is the conscious decision to focus credit provision for business purposes only and only to the selected market segment and thus avoid any form of consumption-based lending and thus be a responsible financier. Such an exclusive focus and specialisation would lend support to the operator to understand its customer needs more deeply and hence fasten the development of a compelling customer value proposition. This comes through client engagement, conducts of intensive research, and the client base surveys and thus uncovering valuable insights associated with a strong niche focus. The in-depth understanding of the subsector linkages in the client segment and the regional nuances enables the development of adapted products that are competitive advantage. For example, research has shown that an MFI which had engaged with this segment intimately for at least 5 years came up with a narrowed down product line that was flexible, unique, and simple that made life easier for the customer and thus enhanced the customer journey experience. Integral to the business's strategic positioning is product innovation. For example, recent innovations in the MFI sector in Kenya have ended up with a Flexi Loan Facility as one of its kind in the market. This was a result of the in-depth knowledge and insights on the needs of the customer segment (in particular entrepreneurs with multiple businesses). Your products need to be continuously evaluated to ensure their relevance, competitiveness and for opportunities for improvement that are aligned to the emerging needs of your target customer needs. Product innovation in terms of features and processes will continually provide a competitive edge for the microfinance business.

Operational efficiency and Technology Leverage

Another important lending business growth strategy involves obtaining and leveraging technology. This should help you to enhance efficiencies in your operations and ensure the strengthening of your customer value proposition. Fully automating the loan origination systems and processes is key to remaining competitive in terms of the cost and time involved in making loan disbursement. In many of the MFIs operating around the globe, the technology to support this automation has been largely developed in-house. The most successful automations have been where the loan agents in the field are enabled to originate loans where the clients are to be found with handheld tablets/smartphones. These gadgets are used to upload the required information and images to a central loan vetting team. This has been found to cut and eliminate redundant manual interactions in the loan processing time from approximately 2 weeks to less than a day, resulting in substantial benefit to the customer. The sustainable MFI will continue to actively leverage on emerging and innovative forms of technology to enhance its business proposition.

The successful MFI provides great customer experience by ensuring that the customer service offered at all levels is consistent and exceptional. The field officers maintain personalised services with the client portfolio they manage and are able to offer not just credit but some level of advisory services as well. As a result of relationship management efforts, a significant number of new clients can be referred by existing clients. It has been reported that up-to more than 50% of customers provide repeat business in well IT enabled businesses.

Credit Processes and Analytics

The successful MFIs have deep knowledge of their micro enterprises and the lower end SME segment. Business analytics have been used in building their competitive value proposition through the strengthening and automating credit risk assessments and analysis such that the pricing and lending process is effective and efficient. This ensures that the inherent risk in sector specific lending is understood and mitigated. For example, a very successful credit only MFI in Kenya had a competitive edge through automating its credit risk assessment process, centralised its vetting systems (unique in the market for credit only institutions) and instituted a quality assurance team to support a robust lending process. It uses information gleaned from the credit reference bureaus in pricing products to help inform the lending decision making process.

An example of a leading MFIs lending origination process

Some of the key elements and differentiators in the credit origination and assessment process of the leading MFI include the following:

i. Loan Officers (LO) located in the branches across the country get clients for loans through targeted marketing and referrals from existing customers. When a prospect confirms interest in the loan and is ready to proceed with the loan application process, LOs first conduct pre-validation assessments at the client's business site (quick initial assessment to assess customer suitability and high-level loan affordability);

ii. With a successfully pre-validation criteria, the LO then carries out a client character assessment based on information from referees, immediate community, close relatives etc. as well as information from the documentation obtained from the client, for example, bank statements and credit reference bureau reports;
iii. The LO then carries out a thorough client affordability assessment to estimate the loan facility size, using the business's financial and performance information that is obtained from the client validated business records;
iv. Once satisfied, the LO then uploads all relevant and required documentation and images onto the handheld tablet (a client App) and sends the uploaded information to the Company's central credit vetting team (through the Client Laon App);
v. The central vetting team (located at the Company's head office) then independently reviews and validates all loans on an end-to-end basis. The reviews are done on the documents, compliance to business rules, character, the affordability data and accuracy of calculations, the security and collateral documents and referees ;
vi. This MFI has adopted a risk-based approach for loan approvals, establishing various approval levels for the vetting team, operations managers and a national approvals committee in accordance with loan level criteria such as amount, industry etc.;
vii. Once approved, loans are disbursed directly to the client or supplier account (as the case maybe) via electronic funds transfer or digitally to a mobile phone verified by both client and vetting team;
viii. The above process, assuming all required documentation is in place can take as little as 6 hours!

This quick turnaround time is of vital importance to the success of this MFI within the target market segment and has proven to be a significant competitive edge, providing the MFI with a significant advantage over its peers.

Chapter 5 FINANCIAL ACCESS IN KENYA

Financial health and inclusion

The country's financial health has been reported to have deteriorated in the last 5-7 years such that less than 1 in 5 adults have ability to take care of basic necessities of life as well as deal with emergencies and invest in securing their future livelihoods. This financial strain is to be found across the demographics of men and women, urban and rural, youth and prime working age adults. The personal goals of individuals have shifted away from future orientation (e.g., education) towards current needs of. For example, food and finding work. The financial health deterioration has also affected the wealthier groups.

On the financial inclusion side, the percent of adults who held a formal financial institution or mobile money account had more than tripled between 2006 and 2021, a rise from 27% to 84%, though the pace of financial inclusion had slowed down to rates of half a percent per annum as compared to the almost 3 percent rates experienced in the early 2000s. This scenario arose mainly due to the declining financial health of Kenyans as expressed in the lack of money to save and the costs of maintaining a bank account reasons. The mobile money account has become the main medium for channelling money. The other key reasons for substituting bank accounts with mobile money are resultant from the Corona virus pandemic (between 2019 and 2021) effects of, the massive closure of branches, the adoption of remote payments as necessitated by the social distancing requirements as well as the reduction in the traction cots on mobile money transactions. The shifts may also have resulted from clients drawing down their funds from relatively higher-cost, relatively illiquid instruments, for example, bank checking accounts and group savings, so as to be able to survive and manage the increased costs, loss of employment and reduced incomes. Quick low-value credit that was flexibility came under high demand pressure following the tightening of the individuals' and families' financial conditions.

The credit landscape to financial health also shifted in like manner as relates to the motivators/reasons for borrowing. Borrowing to fund day to day needs increased from 17 percent to 40 percent between 2016 – 2021 among adult borrowers according to recent findings by the Financial access survey. Emergency based borrowing has risen threefold. The savings versus use cases follow similar trends.

The above coupled with the demographic surveys portend a huge opportunity for providers of credit and other banking type services. The surveys measure the financial inclusion landscape (access, usage, quality and impact) and have shown evidence of significant improvement in enhancing Kenya's financial inclusion, a good indicator towards achieving vision 2030 as well as the Central Government's Medium-Term Plan on financial services. In this section, we provide summaries of the various surveys data and their implications for the sustainability of microfinance businesses. The analysis gives data on key market segments and services uptake drivers.

Demographics

The demographic statistics of Kenyans above 16 years present interesting opportunities for microfinance businesses. According to financial access survey, there's a near balance between female and male adult Kenyans (52%: 48% respectively). In terms of the split between Urban and Rural dwellers, a large percent of the population lives in the rural parts of the country and constitute 63%. More than 70% of the surveyed numbers reported an education level of between primary and secondary school. This cohort will generally be employed in blue color jobs, micro enterprises, and peasant farming. The age distribution shows skews toward the young (below 35 years of age). These will need funding for various reasons including consumption.

There's thus limitless permutations on the product offerings that an MFI can come up with. For instance, you can target women or men exclusively or a combination in varied proportions according to age, education, rural/urban et cetera. There's actually more than enough room for creating either niche or non-niche based profitable MFI models depending on your comfort

Occupation and Consumption Patterns[1]

Agriculture is the dominant income generating activity for livelihoods in the country, but people have at least one additional income source and will mainly be a side hustle/business. This scenario again provides wonderful opportunities for microfinance businesses that can structure financing solutions to varied needs based on occupational activities of communities.

---

[1] All data presented in here was from the FinAccess Surveys

Your sustainable microfinance business guide

Main sources of livelihood

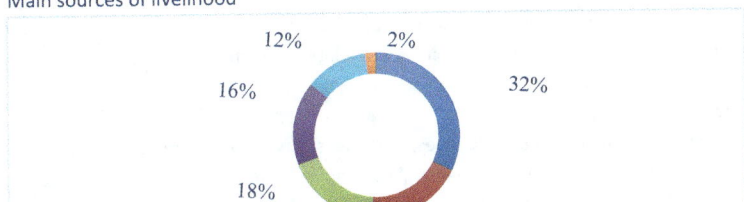

- Agriculture 32%
- Casual work 19%
- Own business 18%
- Dependent 16%
- Employment 12%
- Other 2%

The desire for educating oneself is high among the younger groups while feeding family as a priority increases with age. We can therefore say that non consumption financing is most needed in the younger groups and hence financing solutions towards education and enterprise are most needed by the youth.

How individuals rank their goals

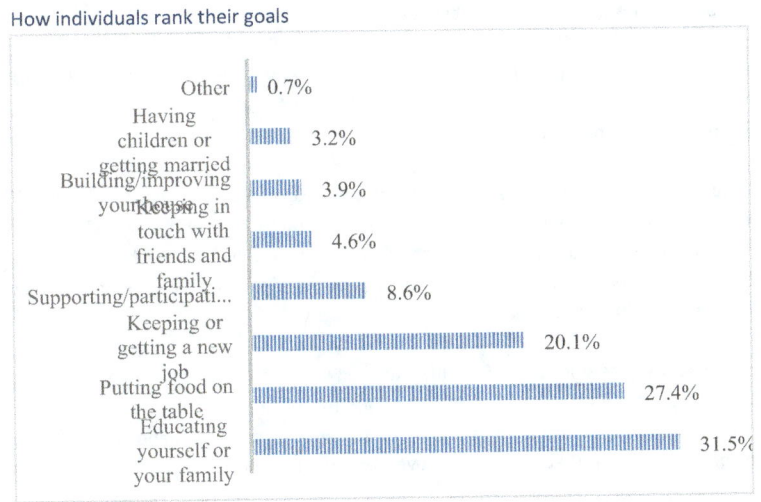

- Other: 0.7%
- Having children or getting married: 3.2%
- Building/improving your house: 3.9%
- Keeping in touch with friends and family: 4.6%
- Supporting/participati...: 8.6%
- Keeping or getting a new job: 20.1%
- Putting food on the table: 27.4%
- Educating yourself or your family: 31.5%

Dealing with Disturbances/Emergencies

The rural population's worst disturbances come from droughts while the urban population experiences shocks coming from relatives' deaths and property losses.

Coping mechanisms
To deal with unforeseen disturbances, personal savings play the major role followed by social networks help. Emergency financing solutions would be welcomed by households. Small investment schemes for individuals and groups will thus be a portend solution to a majority. There have been leaps in the formal financial inclusion of women between 2009 and 2017 with men's inclusion showing a steady rise. Women have been helped by the sprouting of mobile financial services (MFSs). However, women still access less of the regulated space's financial services compared to men.

Access to finance in rural populations has been dwindling while urban populations' access has doubled over the decade. Microfinance businesses have unique opportunities to create financing models for rural communities and reap the benefits while still being sustainable in the Triple Bottom Line measures.

Financing services appear to be concentrated in the median ages and hence leading to exclusion of the young and elderly. There need to be products for these ages. Microfinance pioneers stand to gain big!

Data shows that lower levels of literacy hamper access to credit. Hence, financing of education could serve as a good societal contribution by MFI businesses. More than 98% of persons of post primary education can access formal finance while up to 78% of up to primary education people access finance. Less than 40% of persons without formal education access finance.

About 42% of the poor are financially excluded vis-à-vis a country average of 17.4% whilst more than 90% of the wealthiest access formal finance. Salaried and business people are the most included as compared to agriculturally based and casual labour income earners who report very low levels of formal financial access.

There are region specific variations in formal inclusion and exclusion with more than 70% formal inclusion in most parts of the country where the Western and Coastal regions show a slightly lower level of inclusion. The highest exclusion levels are observed in the northern parts of the country of up to about 52%.

Usage of Financial Services

Mobile financial services are twice preferred to banks and informal mechanisms of accessing and providing financial transactions and in this respect, nearly twice as many Kenyans use mobile financial services thanks to increasing financial inclusion. There has been a spike in the use of most types of financial services, particularly banks and informal groups between 2006 and 2017. SACCOs saw periods of dipping usage owing to preference of union members to physical branch visits but with a surge recently towards acceptance and usage of all the other types.

Mobile financial services, mobile banking and informal groups are the most used on a daily and weekly basis while Banks, MFIs and SACCOS are mostly used once a month. This presents opportunities by micro lenders that can leverage technology to provide mobile based credit to micro borrowers. Of worthy note is that women outnumber men in the use of MFIs and informal financing channels.

Urban areas outperform rural areas in the usage of varied financial services providers and prominently so in banks.

The wealthy are more likely to be financially included than the less wealthy persons. MFIs must therefore fulfil their outreach objectives by tailoring their financial services to the less wealthy for them to achieve their double bottom-line objectives.

The source of livelihood does not restrict the use of mobile financial services but appears to have a little bearing the use of informal groups. Salaried individuals dominate the use of all financial services. Business operators also use all types of services, although less intensively, dominate the use of MFIs and informal sources.

Diversification of financial services usage has become a trend with more than 60% of the population having more than one service type.

Application of Credit

More than 30% of the population uses credit. There's been a demand correction from the dip in 2013. Daily needs and education financing are the key drivers for the demand for credit. SACCOs and informal groups are preferred for education type loans. Business and agricultural financing needs are mostly met from informal groups while everyday needs are met through mobile bank accounts and informal groups.

Wealth significantly affect borrowing behaviour with the wealthy being able to refinance loans while the poorer populations have to liquidate assets to repay a loan.

Access to Financial Channels & Providers

The potential for data services is still being challenged by the infrequent access to the internet as well as lack of smart phones (most likely a cost variable). Approximately 30% of adults are loyal to a particular mobile financial services agent. Besides proximity, trust plays a major role.

Personal savings are the primary source of financing to Bbusiness owners and farmers. Formal credit is very rare especially in agricultural settings.

Chapter 6 OPERATING A MICROFINANCE BUSINESS

Funding your micro-lending business

Introduction

Generally, MFIs can be financed through commercial banks loans, private investor funds (private equity/venture capital), corporate bonds and through customer deposits for those that get licensed to be deposit-taking. There also exist equity investment type of private equity funds that MFIs can attract in exchange for ownership stakes and share in residual profits. The funding profiles available and accessible to MFIs have led to the emphasis of microcredit over savings for many MFIs (existing and new).

Where the MFI industry is highly developed and mature, the funding sources are usually quite diverse compared to nascent markets where borrowing dominates as the primary funding source. At the advent of microfinance, there was a dependency on donor funding, thereby creating a bottleneck to growth as donor funds were niche based, catering to a specific section/geographic area and or gender with a litany of restrictive covenants. Many MFIs then turned to commercial financing sources. This capital source limitation brought forth the following interrelated issues for MFIs:

a. muted and sub-optimal growth rates notwithstanding the abounding opportunities for growth and expansion.
b. huge operational deficiencies until the time when the institution reaches the breakeven point. This in itself tends to limit optimal growth rates which the institution could otherwise reach for. These imposed operating deficits in turn hamper the MFIs ability to access capital, even at market rates.

It is justifiably undeniable that every MFI needs to get access the funding necessary to enable it impactfully contribute to poverty-reduction and eventually alleviation. However, commercial lenders and equity investors (whether private, public or hybrid) continue to be confronted with difficulties in identifying and selecting viable micro-lending businesses to invest in, or do not yet see microfinance with the poor as a potentially profitable investment opportunity. This raises a key question of how an MFI can effectively communicate its prospects and business model to potential mainstream investors to get attention. Here, the development of funding pitch documents becomes crucially important.

Hitherto, MFIs have primarily been funded through direct donor funds, subsidies from governments and debt capital. These traditional finance sources have not been able to close the funding gaps and hence MFIs still continue to search for new classes of potential investors who can participate in their development projects. The next sections now describe the sources of funding in more detail.

Grants and soft credit from donors and governments

Microfinance has and still receives significant attention from the donor community, because of its inherent capacity for impacting poverty alleviation efforts. The more established large MFIs principally source their finance through grants and highly subsidized loans (or so-called soft loans). The main providers of these soft loans are multilateral banks (for instance, the World Bank and the like), government aid agencies (e.g., United States, Agency for International Development (USAID), UK Department for International Development (DFID)), foundations (e.g., The Ford Foundation) and apex organizations (such as Women's World Banking, ACCION, FINCA). Such grants and soft loans come with conditionalities and covenants regarding the uses and applications of the funds and are in limited in the quantum that is available and accessible. However, in their quest to increase their outreach and impact on financial inclusion, MFIs still need to access capital above and beyond grants and soft loans.

Client Savings accounts

Customer deposits form the main funding source for financial institutions, especially commercial banks. These deposits fuel the banks' credit operations. The same client deposits are available for MFIs that are licensed to take deposits as a source of funds. However, in most developing countries, MFIs are required to comply with minimum capital requirements as mandated by regulatory authorities, and hence not all their deposits are available for lending. The downside to this is that the set minimum capital levels cannot be met during the MFI's infancy period. This, therefore, precludes many would-be vibrant MFIs from benefiting from the potential leverage provided by these deposits.

Private Sector funding (Private equity)

Many of the donor microloans programs employ a sort graduated scaling in their lending practices such that repeat loan sizes are stepped up in subsequent borrowings depending on the loan repayment/collection history, and it is therefore very important to raise/attract sufficient funds to sustain this process. This has led to MFIs moving towards the more traditional sources of capital financing available to corporates. The first choice has been debt capital in the form of borrowings from commercial banks, or long-term debt instruments like bonds that the MFIs issue to the public for private investors to buy in. Sometimes this goes as far as an MFI listing its issued bonds on the fixed income segment of the security exchanges.

Equity (Owner Capital)

Certain equity (share capital) and quasi-equity funding structures that can be used and are available to an MFI include:

a) Donations which can be looked at as an equity investment with no donor expectation of profit participation nor repayment of the donated funds,
b) Not for Profit organizations (NPOs) publicly owned take ownership stakes in the MFI as a funding mechanism, with the NGOs participating in the management of the MFI as well,
c) Nonrepayable/noncallable financing provided by venture capitalists and other quasi-equity investments
d) Equity-like subordinated debt private placement funds,
e) Limited partnerships or limited liability company participating institutional or individual investors interested in social returns or impact programs,
f) Classical equity which requires some ROI in the form of future cash flow receipts.

The microfinance funding stages

The table below illustrates the typical MFI funding evolution chronology as it moves towards equity funding. We can see that funding by donors dominates the early-stage financing (Start-up, Operational Self-sufficiency) of the MFI. It is to be noted that the early-stage MFI will have challenges in qualifying for commercial funding of any kind since there lacks the proof of concept and operational capacity. Private debt capital becomes available as the MFI develops into self-sufficiency. Debt funding structures come with restrictive conditions and attach guarantee requirements before accessing the funding. It is only in the last stage of MFI evolution that traditional equity financing will be appropriate and mostly available.

Table 1: Stages of MFI funding

Your sustainable microfinance business guide

	Stage I:	Stage II:	Stage III:		Stage IV:	
	Start-Up	Operational self-sufficiency	Financial Self-sufficiency		Commercial level Return	
Source	NGO	NGO	NGO	Licensed financial institution	NGO	Licensed financial institution
Grants and soft loans	x	x	x	x	x	x
Internal						
Forced savings	x	x	x		x	
Voluntary savings				x		x
Commercial loans		x	x	x	x	x
Guarantee funds		x	x	x	x	x
Bonds			x	x	x	x
Securitization			x	x	x	x
Inter-bank borrowing				x		x
Quasi-equity			x	x	x	x

Retained earnings				x	x	x	x
Socially responsible equity					x	x	
Commercial equity						x	x

Source: hdl.handle.net

Funding Mechanisms Innovation

It takes a while for an MFI to be able to attract serious funding from investors and hence creative efforts have been going on to further develop financial instruments to facilitate the mobilization of funds for microfinance. Some of the financing vehicles created and used in practice include the following:

Credit Guarantees

This is a way of funding that serves to induce funders to extend credit to those retail MFIs that have high prospects for success even though they lack collateral and/or have limited financial history. The guarantee serves as a default security such that the lender claims against the guarantor in the event of payment failure by the principal borrower. A subsidiary function of this guarantee-ship is to bridge the gap between funders and MFIs (clients) and, thereby make banks to extend credit facilities to MFIs that would ordinarily not get bank finance. Illustrations of these kinds of structures include USAID loan portfolio guarantee (LPG) program for the Compagnie Bancaire de l'Afrique Occidentale (CBAO) in Senegal, and the International Finance Corporation (IFC) launch of a Global Credit Enhancement Facility (GCEF) in the early 2000s. Additionally, *"under the Micro and Small Enterprise Development Program, USAID has used innovative financial instruments including guarantees to facilitate lending to buyers of MFIs"* (see hdl.handle.net).

Securitization

This constitutes another innovative attempt to link microcredit institutions with capital markets by creating a special purpose vehicle (SPV) which then buys the microfinances' portfolio and finances itself by issuing debentures for the capital market.

Specialized equity funds

There exist equity funds formed just to provide funding for MFIs development. For instance, Profund, DEVCAP and AfriCap were and continue to be supported by donors to invest in MFIs through the provision of Equity Capital. They both are unique in size and geographical specialization with AfriCap focussing on Africa. DEVCAP provides funding to microlenders by four US based development agencies (Save the Children, Catholic Relief Services, Appropriate Technology International and SEED Capital Development Fund) which in turn finance MFIs in 54 countries. Complementary to these are similar equity investments from international investment companies and examples include, The Triodos-Doen Foundation, founded in 1994 providing equity capital to MFIs across the globe in addition to loans and loan guarantees (see hdl.handle.net).

Capital Raising Strategies

Traditional Approach

This method assumes that the MFI is primarily formed to impact on poverty reduction and therefore targets raising money from donors and philanthropists. The funding proposal will then begin with the description of the MFI that includes MFI background information, the existing product and services offering, the customer segment that is targeted, the intended social impact and the appropriate financing that is being sought. The expected returns to potential investors are usually described in terms of the number of poor people to be served, and the types of impact it will have on the lives of the poor. The MFI will need to demonstrate in its proposal how its financing programs will improve the lives of the poor including how the impact will be measured.

Financial Analysis Approach

The leading funding organization applies financial due diligence procedures to make conclusions and decisions about the appropriate type and size of either an equity or debt investment. Here, the operating cashflows of the MFI play a central role as the own sustainable sources are paramount. The offering memorandum by the MFI must thus provide cogent arguments for its projected cash flows as well as their timing. A full range of other financial information is also required including the balance sheet and income statement (Profit or loss account). Favorable investor response goes to those firms who have put in place proper and sound financial reporting and control procedures.

Establishing a microfinance business

The factors discussed below will inform the decision of MFI market entry and it is imperative that one obtains a thorough grasp of them. This is obviously not a walk in the pack! There are financial resources and human capacity limitations that must be considered and addressed. This therefore calls for the use of existing experiences to enter the market and to provide microlending financial services efficiently and cost-effectively.

The need for research

Extensive research should be the beginning point to implementing an MFI and this should take the form of a feasibility study. There's always the undue pressure to jump in but time taken to prepare for the launch of service will forestall a lot of mishaps and save unnecessary costs of correcting avoidable mistakes. Published research confirms time and again the importance of a feasibility study, however simple the process is. A feasibility study will ensure that all aspects of the potential market are comprehensively examined and that the costs and risks, opportunities, and benefits to expect are mapped out and understood. The following are the key issues to examine:

Client profiling

a. Ensure that the criteria for segmenting the market are well defined and understood. This could be done by loan size, by business segment/sector, by type of product/service etc.
b. Check that customer preferences that are unique are understood and verified, for instance, the types of products clients look for and long for having them, their attitudes and behaviour towards thrift and the form their thrift habits take, for examples, savings in the form of livestock or food stock, etc.
c. Get an clear view of the client level of technology adoption, for example, mobile technology perceptions and use patterns.
d. Comprehend the constraints, bottlenecks and pain points facing the clients' financial access efforts and activities.
e. Get a view of education levels and profiles which have a bearing on product adoption and acceptance.
f. Have a good view of the geographical demographics of clients compared to mobile network coverage.
g. Have a view of the distance from the nearest service location as it affects the costs to financial access.
h. Assess the clients' willingness and ability to pay.

Regulatory Framework

a. Have a grasp of the special licensing, if any, that is required to set up and operate e-/mobile transactions in the country of operation.
b. Check all the existent limits on client maximum exposures and by channel of service delivery, for example, the amounts that can be sent or stored on the e-wallet or mobile money device.
c. Understand client documentation requirements (Know Your Customer).
d. Any other relevant licensing including consumer protection laws.

Processes

a. Define all the processes involved in customer service including sales origination, assessments and appraisals, onboarding, customer data storage, loan disbursements to customers and collections that might require implementing mobile payments or other forms of loan repayments and receipting.
b. Identify computer based systems that require to interconnect, for example, your customer data capturing system and the third-party systems like mobile money systems.
c. For those systems that are automated, the need to define the approvals process.
d. Define and outline the services marketing system.

Competition

a. Obtain a detailed and clear understanding of the competition and benchmark on those considered as the industry's best while adapting the identified benchmarked practices.
b. Adopt and adapt but never copy paste, there's always a better or different way.
c. Find and exploit niche/captive segments.
d. Find blue oceans and implement a blue ocean strategy.
e. Check possibilities for collaboration on a shared system.

Management Information Systems

a. identify the minimum volumes that will be needed before moving from a manual system to open-source applications to core banking systems.
b. Check the break-even points. What is the minimum data that must be captured to service your segment?
c. Identify, consider, and quantify the costs for implementing and integrating your MIS with mobile network operators, banks, or third-party platforms.
d. Define the key performance indicators and their frequency and their comparatives.

Technology

a. Identify and consider the types of gadgets available to clients and their associated cost (phones, tablets, computers).
b. Check the possibility of creating applications in the local language.
c. Check the need for availing interactive voice response services.

Network

Mobile Network Operators (MNOs):

a. Find out how many operators there are in the country and their reach/preference and market shares.
b. Find out the Geographical distribution of the MNOs agents.
c. Find out the tariff's variations and terms.
d. Make comparisons of client transaction fees.
e. Find out if there are additional hardware or software investments.
f. Check for any exclusivity rules and their potential implications to scaling and diversification.
g. Confirm the availability of real-time transactions and reconciliations.

Third parties:

a. Evaluate the fee structure/cost of services of suppliers.
b. Confirm if there are any additional hardware or software implications.

Agent network

Before setting up an MFI, you need to first check and confirm whether there is an existing sales agents' network that you can tap into for your sales program or then decide whether you need to develop your own sales network from scratch. An existing sales agent network will save you brick-and-mortar establishment and running costs.

Where there is an already established agent network:

a. Verify and confirm the number of agent points and their geographical distribution.
b. Obtain and evaluate their incentives frameworks.
c. Verify their liquidity (e-float) management history.
d. Consider and verify the agents' capacity (and willingness) to acquire new clients.
e. Obtain and verify the exclusivity clauses in contracts with the MNO (i.e., whether they are allowed to act as agents for others e.g., mobile money services).

If there is no existing agent network, it is important to understand:

a. The existence of local businesses that can act as retailers for your service (e.g., shops, butcheries, clubs, restaurants, air-time resellers)
b. The training needs of your agents.
c. Incentives needed to become interested in becoming a retail agent and the quality control measures required to be put in place.
d. Whether your loan officers or group leaders can act as agents and use existing infrastructure.

Business model selection

The next decision based on the data analysis from research is the MFI business model type that will be used to go to market. There are likely to be competing choices on the IT platform model as to whether to own or lease, the partnerships to enter into and how many and the criteria of selecting partnerships, including banks and other institutions. The feasibility study should make these choices easier and sound. Research shows that a lot of recent MFIs partner with multinationals or third-party investors, for example mobile money transfer FinTechs. The explanation for this is that, in many instances the multinationals would have certain experiences in Key MFI proposed services like remittance services with trusting clients and therefore the MFI would wish to leverage on the existing network and visibility.

Products and Services

MFIs provide products and services akin to those offered by the traditional banking industry. However, one key difference is the method of delivering them and the scale of these products and services. This notwithstanding, hitherto formalization efforts in microfinance have focused on enterprise lending (loans for enterprise/business firms formation and development commonly known as business finance). Thus, business lending continues to dominate the MFIs product set. This, however, has undergone a metamorphosis with significant developments towards expanding the products sets of MFIs into deposits (savings accounts mainly), consumption or emergency loans, insurance, and business education.

There's an established market need for deposits and insurance services for the low-income communities in addition to the credit products. The point is for MFIs to be innovative and provide tailored credit services for the poor with add-ons of insurance products like credit life and other insurance services and not being rigid in their loan products offering. It is even more worthwhile to take a micro-sectorial approach and develop models of, for instance, small construction management contractors and create a tailored lending structure for small (SME) contractors. It is therefore vitally important that MFIs are acutely client-focused and provide offerings of a mix of financial products tailored to the varied needs and wants of low income consumers and SMEs.

Loan products

The overarching feature in microcredit is the absence or insignificance of the traditional collateral. The requirement of a security as a loan access condition has been an important variable in financial access that has excluded the low income classes. The alternative is the social collateral accorded in group lending type of products. Social collateral introduces joint liability executed through a variety of methodologies. Essentially, a group of borrowers takes over the behavioral management of borrowers that include; deciding who to lend to, the monitoring, and enforcement of loan contracts from the lending institution. The joint liability where each group member is made responsible for the loans of other group members, can also be achieved through guarantor requirements. Defaults by any member triggers a loan servicing transfer responsibility to the co-borrowers or guarantors. Failure to pay guarantees loss of access to future loans as well. Each member safeguards her future interests by ensuring that only good character persons with the ability and willingness to pay borrow with her or are guaranteed by her.

Social collateral also accomplishes its intended purpose through the reputational risk management inherent in persons who consider themselves of good social standing and therefore loan servicing is seen by members of the group as vitally important to keep their status. The effectiveness of this social collateral model has been confirmed by research with the conclusion that *"agents will always form groups with agents of the same type and that agent's types can be distinguished according to the rate at which they are willing to trade increased joint liability commitments for lower interest rates"* (see es.scribd.com)Hence, Group lending not only increases repayment rates and welfare via social collateral, but also due to peer selection by members of the lending group. As a result, lenders who adopt the use of peer-monitoring systems are able to price their services significantly lower compared to the conventional lenders. In addition, even at the same interest rate as the conventional lenders, the expected loan service rate is higher and where peer monitoring is adopted.

It is advisable to segment the MFI loans into both enterprise and consumption/emergency loans (these might include such products as funeral expenses loans depending on how far you want to be innovative and take risk). The consumption/emergency loans have been buoyant in developing countries and have sustained the existence of informal money lenders (though dubbed, often stereotypically, as shylocks who prey on the poor's misfortunes with extreme pricing and unsavory collection methods). These moneylenders still provide value to the poor by infusing liquidity into the immediate consumption smoothing means of these communities of low-income households just as savings solutions are integral to the poor households' risk management and coping mechanisms. The continued existence of a robust demand for moneylenders emanates from the flexibility of the loan-terms such as the speed of loan assessment and eventual approval and disbursements, flexibility in terms, much reduced repayment periods to days or weeks as well as bullet repayments.

Savings schemes

The market for deposit type solutions especially savings accounts remains unexhausted. Deposit taking MFIs have typically offered 2 types of savings accounts forms.

i. The voluntary form that is primarily available for none borrowing participants with small cash inflows that would be spurned by commercial banks. There's growing evidence that the poor too regard savings for unforeseen events as integral to them and thus it has been said that:

"Savings are integral to poor households' risk management strategies; they constitute the first line of defense to help poor households cope with the external shocks, emergencies, and life-cycle events to which they are so vulnerable; and they play a crucial role in allowing the poor to take advantage of productive investment opportunities" (**See es.scribd.com**)

ii. The forced form where the deposit taking MFI's clients are required to maintain accounts with the MFI with routine minimum deposits into the accounts. The accounts come with restrictive rules of withdrawals. The rationale here is that it enforces financial discipline on the part of the clients but in fact MFIs primarily use these as a form of cash collateral and information gathering purposes on the participants.

Insurance services

Health, fire, burglary and life insurance services are being offered by a number of existing MFIs, though not all. These are offered through partnerships with insurance providers with a profit sharing arrangement. Other forms of insurance schemes need to be developed, for instance, crop and livestock insurance. There's empirical evidence that the availability of agricultural type insurance schemes have increased loan repayments for rural based credit institutions. The flow of credit also rises where framers are insured.

Integrative approaches

The integration of non-financial services (e.g., education, funeral expenses) with financial services remains largely untapped. Integrated services have been known to improve family health and business management skills hence high ability and willingness of customers to pay loans. Including business related training in an MFI's services significantly improves microenterprise performance and the empowerment of microbusiness owners.

Another integrative approach involves providing equity and startup capital in lieu of debt for the formation of enterprises

Your microfinance business' success

According to an article by Bhatt and Tang in which they discuss MFI vehicles, technologies, and performance assessments, there's a consensus that the future success of microfinances' will be determined by the MFI design tailored to specific clients. Sound practices of MFI design and management must therefore be developed to ensure an MFI's sustainability. Hence, the key best practice areas entail:

i. Setting an optimal lending interest-rate,
From a purely commercial perspective, interest rates are set such that shareholder returns are maximized. However, as we already saw, MFIs have double bottomline objectives and therefore face unique issues in setting an appropriate rate. Too high rates cause or exacerbate the financial exclusion problem. Furthermore, extreme high rates are known to increase the probability of loan repayment defaults and, in the case of group lending, bog down their solidarity groups. However, because the principal amounts lent in microcredit and hence little scale economies to cover non variable costs and the fact that MFIs operations involve high administrative per unit costs, to achieve financial self-sufficiency, high rates are invariable and unavoidable.

ii. Determining your lending target (groups or individuals),
We saw earlier that the microcredit industry places significant reliance social collateral within loan groups loan security. Studies show positive relationships between group lending and the presence of neighbors with self-employment earnings. This implies that loanees with higher earnings will have an easier time of servicing their microloans. The design of group lending is also important, and its success depends on MFI lending policies, cost structures, nature and extent of social relations among group members, and MFI staff.

In spite of the dominance of group loans in worldwide micro lending, individual loans are significant in a number of places and have been increasing in popularity. The features that allow micro lenders penetrate new market segments like individual lending include direct monitoring, regular repayment schedules, and the use of non-refinancing threats.

In summary, all formal and informal financial services providers give credit at a price called the interest rate. Traditional banks quote this interest rate on an annual basis on the reducing balance. MFIs and other money lenders quote a flat rate method which tends to reflect the rate as lower although this is not in fact the case.

iii. The management

The current empirical data supports the thinking that efficient MFI management has a positive bearing on the propensity to achieving microfinance objectives. The imperative is therefore putting in place a committed, trained, qualified, motivated, loyal, and visionary management team. Such a team cannot be put together and sustained without some form of longterm commitment to the MFI, particularly with some form of equity interest via an employee share ownership program (ESOP).

Credit Underwriting Models

There are two main credit underwriting models to consider. These are: i) The Group-lending model where the borrowers are organized as groups and/or where informal groups are used to achieve economies of scale from the small sized transactions and instituting group guarantee mechanisms; and ii) Character-based credit appraisal where loan applications are assessed and approved based on the borrower character, rather than traditional collateral (ownership of land or other assets) and viability of projects to be financed; and iii) Focus on micro-enterprises: a special focus on financing very small businesses and the poor.

Loan Collection models

The financial sector has always to deal with loan arrears (usually referred to as past due accounts). However, the continued rise of these accounts is a survival problem for lenders. Though collections is often seen to be an activity to be engaged in only at the end of the credit cycle, it is in fact central to lending. MFIs have of late sought to build new and more effective collections strategies due to the industry-wide emphasis on credit promotion and analysis as well as the dynamics of the MFI operating environment.

The Role of Collections

Collections is a crucial service that ensures client maintenance and freeing of cash flows for onward lending. It thus plays a strategic role key to managing client behaviour and a loan servicing culture among clients. The process is also said to be a business activity primarily aimed at producing returns for the institution and converting losses into income.

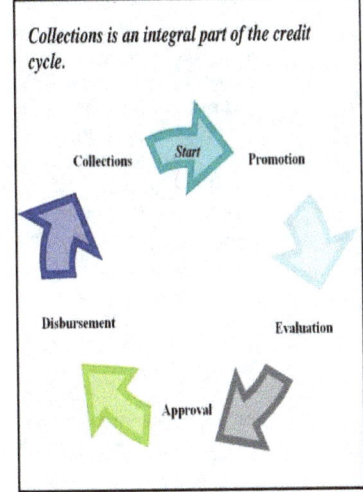

Collections is an integral part of the credit cycle.

MFIs need to thus make collections an integral part of the credit cycle. In the course of the collections process, feedback on policies and activities within each sub-process of the lending cycle (i.e., promotion, evaluation, approval, and disbursement) is obtained and applied appropriately.

The cause of loan delinquencies in Microfinance Institutions

Loan delinquencies have their origin in the underwriting process. A lot of the delinquencies are avoidable with proper loan origination controls. The common errors in lending sub-processes that take place before collections include:

a) Promotion
   Loan delinquencies arise at this stage when the following obtains:
   i. the product does not meet clients' real needs or insufficiently does so.
   ii. lack of clarity on the target client who is just vaguely defined.
   iii. client use of the loan does not match foreseen uses of the loan funds included in the product definition.
   iv. there is no emphasis on a "long-term lending relationship" based on prompt loan servicing.
   v. loan officers, credit agents, promotion officers, etc., lack the requisite training.

b) Evaluation

i. The method applied in credit appraisal fails to identify red flags, including loan amounts that are way above a clients' capacity to pay and over-indebtedness.
ii. The client has a poor quality of references or a questionable attitude towards timely loan repayment.
iii. Poor and insufficient verification of information for consistency as well as poor documentation control.
iv. Inexistant and or unclear loan renewal policies and procedures.
v. No risk-management tools that can aid in making improvements in the understanding of the client probability of default in order to uncover the environmental causes that impede the proper collections of the outstanding loan, and to bring to the attention of management those events of default as well as the those that drive the weak identification of operational risk for instance frauds, weak infrastructure, and gaps in the processes.

c) Approval
   i. Loan approvals decisions suffer from the inherent biases in the pressures to meet sales goals.
   ii. Loan decisions that suffer from subjectivity such trust levels in the loan officer concerned because of experience and loyalty without an established objective credit analysis criteria/policy.

d) Disbursement
   i. An objective analysis not being carried out in order to determine the best loan disbursement conditions including the amount of disbursement, the tenure and installment, frequency, and choice of the repayment date.
   ii. Low client motivation for timely servicing resulting from ambiguous payment instructions and expectations on disbursement date.
   iii. Limited payment channels options. The alternatives may include the Internet-payment options and third-party agents, that could lower client transaction costs.
   iv. Errors arising during operations for example, account holder identification failures, incomplete and erroneous execution of loan documents, and late loan disbursements that makes the client miss the opportunities and purposes for which the loan was intended hence misapplication of funds.

In addition to the sub-processes errors, high loan non performing rates may also arise from an overall lack of collections preplanning and preparedness. Collections is often taken to be a secondary afterthought or, in some cases, nonexistent activity without a defined strategy. Loan dropout rates may also result from external factors outside an MFI's control, such as general sectoral problems, social concerns, illness, theft, fraud, natural disasters and Acts of God, and other emergencies.

When MFIs notice that there has been a loan delinquency rate, they have to analyze the arrears loan portfolio carefully and granularly so that the underlying reason for the arrears is known and the probability of repayment is quickly established. The most effective and efficient collections strategies should immediately be identified as well.

The Collections Process

The whole process of ensuring that the loaned funds are paid back by the client and receipted by the lender is termed the collections process. The involved activities are coordinated, appropriate, and timely with the focus being on the full collection of outstanding loans from clients. All in all, the intent is to convert the MFI's receivables into liquid assets as quickly and efficiently as possible. This process is followed while ensuring that the goodwill of the client for possible future transactions/business is not compromised through unconscionable practices that either embarrass or hurt the client in any way.

Therefore, the collection process by necessity involves interacting with the client in a very significant and intentional manner. The beginning point is a client situation analysis followed by repetitive contact with the client in timely intervals over the loan term. In this process, it helps when clients are presented with appropriate and timely options for loan payments. The collection activities need to be well documented including recordings of the monitoring activities with outcomes for each activity. Compliance to client-agreed on commitments needs to be monitored and follow-up regularly.

Some typical collections activities are described below, followed by a flowchart illustrating a typical collections process.

a) Begin with an analysis of each particular case ensuring you obtain clear answers to these questions: Who the client is, that is, the client's legal identity, occupation etc.? What is his situation, that is his main source of livelihood, his/her household economics, and demographics? Were the original loan conditions complied with and were they appropriate to ensure compliance and follow through? What are the causes of the loan default? Consider internal and external sources of information such as credit bureaus and bad debtors lists in reviewing the client file status.

a) The follow up step is to get into contact with the client and answer the following questions: What information is the client giving out? What is the client's current location? What actions have been taken so far and what have been the results?

b) Next prepare an assessment report that provides answers to these issues: What is the root cause of the current default? What is the client's true characteristics, willingness and ability to pay?
c) Make the case for alternative resolutions: What options are available to resolve the delinquent account? The intention should be to provide incentives for timeous settlement of the account to foster a positive payment culture with the client.
d) Work to get to the client making payment commitments: Are the negotiations effective and thus producing the desired results? There must be a clear identification of the time and date, as much as is possible, the method and amount which the debtor has committed to make a payment. It is also crucial to must remember, for example, how a client in a situation of over-indebtedness or decreased income will prioritize the payment of his bills. Is it possible to get the client to commit to prioritizing repayment of this loan?
e) Monitoring payment commitments compliance: Did the client honour past commitments in both amount and time? Does the client show that he is actually interested in repaying the loan? The important idea here is to observe and ensure consistency throughout the collections process. Getting client commitments then depending on his apparent goodwill and positive attitude is not enough and so collections staff must make follow up efforts on these payment commitments.
f) Check that the recording of collections activities is adequate: Is there a coordinated and consistent collections activities that is being observed and followed through? Can you put yourself in the position of the collections member next in line for collections activities with that client and come to the same conclusion as is?
g) Case follow up: Is the client's situation and the collections activities the case visible to all involved including the most seniour person?
h) Intensify the collections activities by getting clarity on the best action available to secure collections of the loan in the most immediate manner. Find out the assets, if any, the client owns and what can be collected through legal action. At this point, the loss of the client is not part of the equation but recovery of the outstanding.
i) Loss definition: There needs to be in place a loan loss policy that defines the criteria of determining when a loan is no longer collectible and thus stop any further deployment of resources on collection and thus a credit is deemed a loss.

The Collections Process diagram

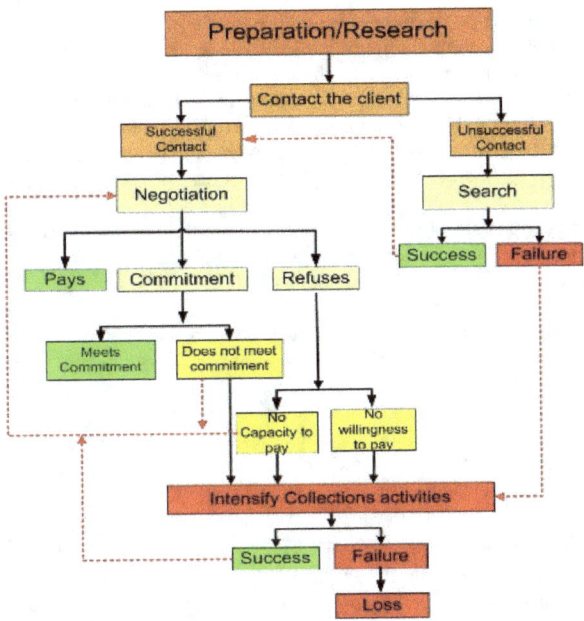

Source: www.microfinancegateway.org

The collections process should be seen in the eyes of the client as a continuous rather than a sporadic activity. Hence, the importance of the collections' participants to
—such as call centers, loan officers, and collections agents—acting together in a coordinated and timely manner cannot be overemphasized. The client must see and understand the collections team's engagement continually, acting fast and in an agile manner, and overtly in control of the situation. It is also reiterated that all collections activities should be directed at all persons involved in the loan—including spouse, guarantors, family, or friends who provided references.

A collection process that is not clearly defined, that is haphazard, not well understood by all potentially ends up being inadequate, costly and a total failure. Among the recurring errors in collections are:

a. A high appetite for facility restructuring, refinancing or issuing a new additional loan in order to settle an already problematic facility/loan. This is often done devoid of a detailed and objective analysis and understanding of the circumstances surrounding the client's current conditions. This practice's effect is the temporal masking of the of the true and fair condition of the problematic portfolio but eventually shows up much worse. A refinancing request must be a totally fresh client file evaluation as though it was a new loan and thus subjected to a complete and objective analysis. It should not and cannot be applied as a general strategy or campaign, which do not change payment behaviors. It is also important to note when such a policy might be appropriate (e.g., natural disaster, market fire—when a whole subset of clients has been affected).

b. The unconscionable actions of seizing client goods from the business or home. This more often than not distracts the collections activities from the main responsibility and thus turns into something akin to an intermediary or salesperson activity. It creates unnecessary and unplanned storage and administration costs on the seized items and sends the wrong signal to the client with respect to the client's financial obligations as oftentimes the client would elect to lose the assets without trying to repay the loan, thus weakening the institution's position and image/reputation in the market.

c. Tendency to be subjective. Considering certain clients and cases as a total loss or placing too much trust in the goodwill of the client can detract from the collections process and lead to a loss of time and money for the institution.

The crucially important matter to understand is that the long-term sustainability of an MFI is dependent on it recognizing the peculiarities of its clients and therefore each of the collection activities requires a considerable investment of time, money, and effort from the different parties participating in collections. It is much easier to keep an existing client than to create and attract a new one.

Best Practices in Collections

Healthy, sustainable growth results require that MFIs put together collections strategies before new products or programs are launched. We discuss below some "best practices" for collections. These practices are operationalized well before the loan is delinquent, in an attempt to craft proactive strategies to forestall the occurrence of loan arrears and recognize the crucial part internal and external collections staff play. They provide ideas for precise data collection and maintenance, client segmentation and offering of "collections products" or payment alternatives tailored to the needs of the client. And, finally, they suggest a list of policies and procedures leading to successful collection of problem exposures.

1. Put in place proactive strategies that prevent loan delinquencies beforehand

Anticipating and forestalling problems in advance is proven to be the most effective and efficient practice in collections to cut down on loan delinquency. It is often stated that loans that are not yet past due are the easiest to correct at an instance of an early warning sign and thus keeping a performing account performing through continuous client situation analysis is the best practice number one in collections. The following strategies can be employed in this case before clients' loans are due:

a) All loanees must be informed and educated in the product features and all the consequential fees and charges to be borne by them

Informationally empowered loanees are known to be the best payers and thus with very low default rates. This, therefore, means that client and guarantor education about the loan products and the loan covenants prior to disbursement is of mandatory importance. The borrower education and training should also include the implications of taking the loan, its workings once it is taken, the benefits of timely payments as scheduled as well as information about the closest and easiest way for this particular client to make loan payments. All collections process related costs are client borne. This should be stressed in the client education programs. This is sometimes packaged as a "reward for punctual payment," offering discounts.

b) Put in place payment dates that are convenient for the client and mutually agreed

The probability of repayment increases when the client is involved in setting up the repayment dates as the client is best placed to know when it is convenient for him/her. This repayment date should correspond to the time of revenue or liquidity gluts in the client's economic cycles. At the same time, it should be far enough away from payment dates for other important obligations, such as rent, school fees, and other debts.

c) Put in place a superior customer-service front desk that addresses complaints fast enough

It is well known that when the product sold to a client sometimes turns out to be defective and/or the client did not receive adequate customer service from the supplier, the result is the cessation of client payments. Paying timely attention and resolution of client complaints may be able to address clients' concerns before they result in a late payment. Sometimes the fast dealing with client complaints unearths situations that could be the result of fraudulent staff action, etc. In this case the MFI must analyze the situation and, if it determines that late payment is due to problems with the product or service, propose a timely solution in order to "reactivate" the client.

d) Positively reinforce good payment behaviour

Positive reinforcement, though looking obvious, is very valuable. The MFI can recognize and reward timely-paying clients through offers of quick renewals, increased loan amounts, preferential (lower) interest rates, certificates of good payment, training, and prizes. These actions should become embedded and therefore part and parcel of the sales strategy.

2. Improve Internal Productivity of the Collections area

The effectiveness of a collections unit is wholly dependent on the people involved in the process. In designing collections strategies, consider the institutional SWOT analysis where considerations of collections outsourcing is a viable option given a cost-benefits analysis outcome. A review of the measures to be instituted to ensure proper staff training, motivation, and performance measurement should also be done when it is considered that an internal collections team is ideal. An ideal collections process should promote healthy competition among the collections participants. The following form a critical part of this best practice:

a) Identify and chose the appropriate collections procedures

Successful collections activities require a substantial amount of resources to implement. These resources include not just time but money and human capital as well. Microcredit institutions can chose between outsourcing their collections to a specialized collections agency or build its own internal collections unit. This choice must be made after a thorough analysis of available resources, the costs, and benefits associated with each option and the availability of such competent collections' agencies in the market. The following section list potential advantages and disadvantages of both.

Option 1: Outsourcing to Collections Agencies

Advantages

- Collections agencies can afford to train and specialize. This then means that their personnel can be able to dedicate the appropriate time and focus exclusively to collections activities.
- Ability to transfer control and management of collections activities to the agency hence cost savings of time and money.
- The agency has the capacity and the flexibility to try out a variety of collections approaches, such as call centers, collectors, on-site collections agents, and collections points.

Disadvantages

- Inadequate and/or lack of experience of collections agencies in the low-income microloans sector.
- No incentive for client relationships maintenance interest hence creating difficulties in client "reactivation".
- Possible duplication of efforts or contradictions in client presentations.
- Direct client contact by the collections agency may create the impression to the client that MFI is facing challenges and may also result in a loss of confidentiality.
- Challenges in external collections agents complying with the same ethical standards as promoted by the MFI when dealing with clients.

Option 2: Creating an Internal Collections Unit

Advantages

- Tendency of inhouse operations having informational advantages on the client and the market.
- Inhouse units build and keep client relationships that ensure future business referrals.
- Advantages of internal feedback on the whole lending process to strengthen credit processes.
- Staff will be more committed to the organization and to its objectives and therefore aid in brand promotion.
- The MFI's internal database holds information for the development of predictive collections.
- The MFI retains control over the client interface, thus having more direct control over the client ensuring collections practices remain in line with institution's ethical standards.

Disadvantages

- Internal units lack the expert training that specialty collections agencies have. The related costs of management and control are also prohibitive.
- Poor personal and professional recognition for collections staff as collections is perceived as not enjoyable and inhumane.
- Potential distractions from product promotion and analysis activities, especially during periods of expansion.
- MFIs have little experience in collections.

b) Select and Train Staff Members

After choosing between having an internal collections unit or using an external agency, the position and roles in the collections process need to be identified, if any, that are to be filled internally and picked accordingly on the basis of appropriate profile for each position. The roles and responsibilities of each participant in the collections process (e.g. field agents, call center, collections agencies, attorneys) need to be clearly defined including the exact levels of participation. For instance, call-center staff may contact the customer, but should not be allowed to negotiate payment, as they are not trained to take on this task and may lack the background and strategic considerations. The importance of training in achieving successful loan collections and good customer service cannot be overemphasized. The crucial training areas to staff members include techniques and strategies, such as dealing with the typical arguments of the delinquent loan customer, dealing with difficult people, types of clients in existence, communication tips and cues, the typical non-performing loan customer profile, and basic negotiation approaches. In addition, MFIs must ensure their staff members properly understand the correct application of collections tools and knowledge of relevant legal resolutions.

c) Implement Staff Incentives Programs

Incentives motivate staff to apply their talents towards achieving desired results i.e. enhancing collections effectiveness strategies and workplace play to win. Typical incentive programs are based on collections results activities, in terms of percentages of past-due amounts at each different stages of loan performance. A basic system of "commission for collections" could be designed to include higher commissions for the collections of more problematic loans. Incentive programs are traditionally monetary but in-kind incentives can also be designed taking cognizant of the suitability in a given environment.

Another approach to incentives is to design it based on the targeted levels of impairments and thus an incentive is given based on the percentage reduction in the level of monthly provisions. It is important that the parameters that define performance are clearly set out and outlined in an incentive scheme to reward collections' success. Loan delinquency early warning signs should be used so as to prepare for delinquency. Some of the early warning signals could include measures such as a PAR (portfolio at risk) of 1 day or 2,3, and 5 days, rather than the traditional PAR of 15, 30, and 60 days. Earlier delinquency targets and parameters will assist the collections team set a zero delinquency tolerance culture/aspiration. In addition, such early warning signals contribute in identifying past-due loans much earlier where the possibility of healing of delinquent loans is higher during early stage. It will also help remove the temptation and reality of masking an increase in delinquency through portfolio growth, allowing immediate actions to take place.

3. Quality Information Gathering and Management

Loan collections success has been linked to the ability of any lending institution to have visibility of client data and especially around the delinquent client's loan situation and important information that bring feedback about the credit cycle. To achieve this, an MFI must:

a) Institute efficient and effective managing information systems

Fast and cost effective information production systems are essential in facilitating the analysis of collection activities which in turn help in monitoring the evolution of the arrears. The production and circulation of specific and accurate reports is very key in the loan collection process. The following key reports are the minimums expected:

- Management reports that include lists of past-due clients to visit by loan/collections officer, list of past-due clients by amount and days past due, or daily collections report, used by field collections officers to follow up with clients. These should be produced daily at the minimum.
- Monitoring reports that include arrears portfolio by product, collections efficiency ratios, and portfolio analysis by ageing and location. These are used by management to analyze and address issues in nonperforming portfolio performance. These reports should be produced weekly or monthly at the minimum.
- Risk-Management reports, which monitor the impact of collections on loan performance through the tracking of indicators for normalization, billing cycles, recoveries, and loan roll rate ratios. These can be produced daily for tracking seasonality or monthly for forecasting purposes and performance management.

The MIS adopted keeps historical records of actions and collection activities already undertaken. This is particularly important where there are many different channels for collections, for example, loan officers, collections agents, call centers, collections campaigns, etc. as it ensures no breaks in collections activities and therefore continuity carried out by each participant. This in turn avoids duplication of efforts and contradictions.

b) Ensure that client information is of the utmost high quality

Just as we consider the contact details of the client to be important in the enablement of an effective collections process, the collection and collation of quality client information is key in assuring the success of locating a client. The pieces of information including the customer's full name, address, clear narration on how to locate the client (map of location), telephone number, and personal and commercial references should be obtained at the initial loan application stage. This same information should be verified and updated at each step in the collection process so as to facilitate easy client contact. The tools and procedures for updating client information in the database should be put in place with secure access and quality controls.

c) Set up an internal loan arrears collections committee

Members of this b would include staff involved in the collections process, including loan officers, collections agents, and branch managers. The committee should hold meetings for discussing and analyzing specific past-due loan accounts and the possible collections reactions and processes. The committee needs to make suggestions for participants to learn from the errors identified in the evaluation and approval process/phase. The committee also discusses and analyzes portfolio statistics, performance metrics challenges and achievements. This committee may be useful in developing good collections practices and giving feedback to management on the MFI's collections strategies, policies, and procedures as well as helping in delinquency control, demonstrating good decision-making practices, and acting as the appropriate forum for learning/training from the field.

d) Institute internal controls

Best-performing MFIs create internal methodological control units to address the problem of the often lack of a monitoring and control system for the specific products and services of the microfinance industry. In the MFI setting, loan assessments are usually done through a report in lieu of formal banking sector documentation. The credit analysis report is generated by a field loan officer. It provides detail information on the client's family and business situation. This was adopted by MFIs as the traditional banking-sector audit systems have proven to be inadequate for the microfinance industry. This thus increased the motivation for internal audit units to monitor not only the collections process but address all sub-processes of the lending cycle. Methodological control tools are used to keep management apprised of the quality of operations in the branches and the correct application of credit policies and processes. They thus prevent deviations from the established methodology that could potentially have a negative impact on portfolio quality.

4. Develop Well-Defined Strategies for Collections of Delinquent Loans

In order to build an effective working collections mechanism, you need to define and document in a very clear the policies and procedures that will give guidance to your team through the process of collecting. These should also be able to instruct them on how to respond in particular situations. The following are the various strategies that should be included in such policies and procedures.

a) Create policies for making client contact

Define when initial contact ought to be made and the best means (whether by telephone, email, postal service, or visits). This should be determined having considered the cots to benefit analysis outcomes of each available method based on the number of days past-due and the probability of total debt collections. The client-contact policies may include preventive strategies, that include, for instance, payment reminders, and should as well embed a plan that defines the future contact dates and the steps collections process steps to be adhered to.

b) Risk-based collections

The collections process requires making decisions on the timing of client contact, the approach to the client, the appropriate offering, the unkept promises resolution approach, the untraceable client approach, dealing with tragedies or disasters, and many others that are impossible to wholly delegate to the experience of a loan officer. The risk-based collections strategies come in in such cases to provide valuable tools to be selected from for the decision-making process. To deploy a risk-based collections strategy, the following needs preparation:

- A comprehensive analysis and review of information that is available from regulations, the competitive environment, the target market segment, etc.
- Designing the database that will lend support to the deployment of the risk management reports that will be needed for performance monitoring as well as for the building of collection decision support tools.
- Risk management and collections strategy definitions training of the staff involved
- Defining the tool to calculate the client risk levels, whether that client is recoverable, and the best strategy for recovery.

The beginning tool for identifying the client's probability of default is data mining. Alberto Teskiewicz defines data mining as:

"The process of identifying significant correlations, patterns and trends that are hidden among the wealth of information in the database, through the combination of statistics, mathematics, and recognition of patterns. It is an interactive process that allows the institution to convert data into knowledge, generating benefits that translate into lower costs and higher income."

MFIs can be able to forecast loan recovery probabilities through data mining and they can also obtain a score that can be used to prioritize loans in arrears on the basis of their healing probability.

The MFI would develop segmented collection strategies when done with client segmentation based on their repayment probabilities. It does this while optimizing its financial, human and infrastructure resources. Developing the repayment probability forecasting score, the optimized collections strategies and the correct implementation and monitoring of the defined strategies determine the success of the risk-based collections approaches. These strategies have become a common practice in consumer credit (individual credit) but are still nascent within the microfinance sector.

c) Segmentation (attribution analysis)

Client segmentation collection methodology takes cognizant of the fact of uniqueness of each client both in the person and their reasons for delinquency. For client segmentation to be effective, we need to properly identify the delinquency causality factors and classify clients based on attitude, ability to pay, solvency and location. This approach is viewed as an added layer on the risk-level determination (data mining or score-based methodologies discussed above).

Conclusion

Prior to launching any new credit program, an MFI must consider collections given that it is a customer service function that is crucial to the success of the business. Collections is central to the overall lending cycle and provides valuable feedback information on the processes preceding collections. The fallacious popular belief is that loan defaults start at the point when a payment is missed. However, in many cases, the truth is that it is the processes themselves that are the original catalysts of loan payment defaults. The preceding presented best practices, while not exhaustive as strategies employable to address and reduce delinquency, are the most effective, from the author's research and experience. It is important to have the awareness of the consumer protection concerns relating to collections as well as the appropriate cost structure in place to ensure appropriate allocation of funds.

The take home here is that excellent collections strategies should begin before there is a loan default problem.

Chapter 7 MICROFINANCE PERFORMANCE MONITORING

This is a short chapter that chiefly displays the critical things that every MFI operator must keep an eye on to run an MFI efficiently and effectively. They serve as early warning signs of trouble ahead, a rea mirror view of how things have turned out so far and point to the triggers that need to be either maintained or changed for the MFI to remain sustainable. The following snapshots show they key figures and metrics that an MFI management report should include, beginning with an executive summary that captures salient maters around that month's achievements, the challenges faced, the risks and opportunities discovered.

Executive summary

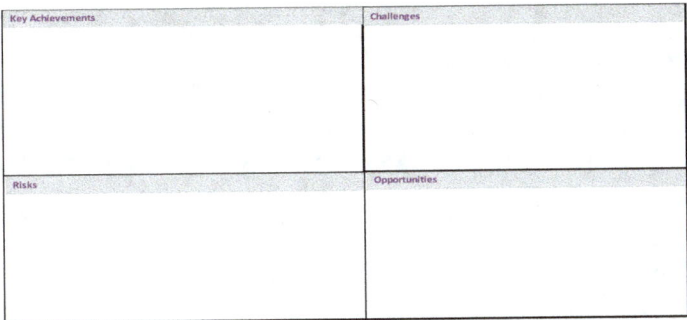

The above could be covered in the Chief Executive's report as illustrated below.

Sample month review report

Month Under Review

3.1. Sales

3.1.1.1. Challenges

Internal

- Sub-optimal agent numbers and productivity - we have struggled get to the target agent number of 180. We ended at 162, but still more than 15 of them have exited (a no show). 107 of the 162 field agents disbursed a deal (a 66% output). The rollover business has been low partly because agents discourage clients from rolling over and instead take them to competition at a higher commission rate (because the loan is considered new by competition). We identified this from some client payslips where new loans have been added from competition, but the clients had declined to take top-ups from us.
- Regressed performances by some regions: Mombasa and Kisumu regions which have, in the last few months performed well, recorded reduced disbursements in June which smothered improved performances by Nairobi and Eastern regions. This is attributed to the "feeding frenzy" on new health workers recruits in the Ministry of Finance that has since ended with the regions not having built a prospects pipeline from the other employers (due to low activations).
- Incomplete understanding of the value proposition and/or positioning of the Flexiloan product: some regional teams seem to have little grasp of the competitive advantages of the product and have thus not been marketing it on same, particularly the credit limit aspect of the product. The result has been that unnecessary documentation is asked where it shouldn't have thus elongating the origination process and possibly TATs.

External

- The current predominantly agent-based business model is no longer in step with the market. With Banks and SACCO's having adopted same business model coupled with their more attractive product propositions (cost, tenor), we are being crowded out. This is seen in the banks inbound settlements that have been on the increase in the recent past.
- Very low brand awareness (the target market still doesn't even know of us or who we are).

3.1.1.2. Corrective Action

- Agent recruitment drive through social media ads and existing agent referral scheme put in place. The retraining of regional teams is ongoing on the Flexi-loan innate advantages. We propose for rollover agent commission to revert to the 7% and eliminate the NBV portion.
- One mass messaging campaign done on Radio Citizen.
    - Campaign generated enquiries of 7,388 prospects through WhatsApp, SMSs, Email and Direct Calls as shown below:

Whats App Reach	51%	3,758
SMS Reach	37%	2,741
Infoemail Reach	3%	234
Call In	9%	655
	100%	7,388

- Prospects analysis: ~ 4,366 (59%) were outside the target market, ~1,361(17%) were civil servants of which only 98 (1%) had affordability on the payslips and ~ 1,661 (22%) were of unknown segment as they did not pick follow up calls.

	Called In	INFO EMAIL	SMS	WhatsApp	Grand Total	%
Non-Civil Servants	578	175	2,112	1,501	4,366	59%

Civil Servants - No ability to pay	64	50	596	553	1,263	17%
Civil servants - With ability to pay	13	9	33	43	98	1%
Unknown-Never picked call backs				1,661	1,661	22%
Grand Total	655	234	2,741	3,758	7,388	100%

- 28 deals worth Kshs 2.86 million have been closed out of the 98 that qualified (29% close rate). The reasons for non-closure identified were:

- Product adjustment proposal to enhance competitiveness drafted for TAC review.

3.1.1.3.   Successes Gained
- A little improved performance in June with disbursements increasing by 10% to 42.8M from 38M in May. Eastern region achieved 124% of target while Nairobi region had an improved performance achieving 88% of target.
- 25% of the loans were to existing clients while 75% were to new clients.
- Net settlements: Net settlements reduced slightly from 26.8M in May to 23.5M in June. However, there was a reduction in buy offs from 2.6M in May to 1.7M in June. The reduction in buy offs was due to delays in obtaining clearance letters from 3rd party for deals which had already been submitted and closure of some payrolls which made it impossible to confirm ability at payrolls. Off Select settlements were mainly by commercial banks which took advantage of their lower interest rates and longer tenures to target our clients.
- Call Centre: The agents were mainly involved in the radio campaign where they were calling the clients who had made inquiries and referring them to the nearest branch for prospect follow up. The agents still managed to disburse 20 deals valued at 1.1M with the two more experienced agents contributing 19 deals while the new agent who is only just settling in closing 1 deal.

3.1.2.   Collections

3.1.2.1.   Major Challenges

- Delayed funding from the counties by the Exchequer continues hampering timely remittance of payments from the counties' payrolls hence substantial outstanding payments from these employers
- First-time defaulters were 67 loans – 47 accounts were due to outstanding payments, but arrears are now cleared, 7 accounts due to outstanding payments, 7 accounts - due to salary stopped – absence from duty, 3 accounts – due to delay by payroll to upload deduction, 1 account – Deceased, and 2 accounts – clients no longer working for an employer (1 Retired and 1 Resigned).
- FID – Were 185 accounts, a drop compared to the previous month - 156 accounts were due to outstanding payments, 19 accounts were due to delay by payroll to upload our deductions, 8 accounts - due to outstanding payments but arrears already cleared,2 accounts - due to delayed June'21 byproduct
- By-product collection - 96% had been received as at the 5th July, an improvement noted compared to the previous month. The byproduct collection remains steady at 96% achieved against the target. Follow-ups being done, with the payroll officers to ensure the byproducts are submitted.

3.1.2.2.   Corrective Actions taken

- 52 -

- Continuous follows ups being done daily with all county CFOs to ensure strong relationships are built, and our payments are prioritized once disbursements are received from the National government.
- Monthly follow-ups ongoing to ensure all clients who drop off the payroll and are either non-performing or partial performing are followed up and installment increased. For the partial performing accounts and non-performing accounts, special campaigns being done by the Call Centre, to call these customers and push for a payment plans as they establish the reasons for the drop-off and arrange for a PTP plan.
- All first-time default accounts have been followed up by the Call Centre team. The physical trace is ongoing for all customers whose salaries have been stopped and demand letters being issued to help build pressure and kick start the collection process.
- For Deceased clients, next of kin called for copies of the death certificates and insurance has been notified.
- Physical trace being done, by the regional collectors to ensure the collection process is adhered to and all accounts are followed up and traced.

3.1.2.3. Successes Gained

- Kshs 10.6M prior outstanding payments were collected
- 47 Restatements were done in June 2021 with provisions of KES 755,859.52 cured.

3.1.3. Operations

3.1.3.1. Challenges

- OTP non-receipt by clients.
- Agents unable to edit new banking details for rollovers loans in instances where client has changed banking details from the existing Sacco/bank details that were previously maintained on the ILS. After picking the new Sacco details, both previous and the current banking details appear on ILS.
- Poor connectivity and unavailability of IPRS system occurred (All our IPRS accounts were in a suspended status-expired) which slowed down production and disbursements in some instances.
- A few deals having an error of finalization greater than threshold or finalization occurs before loan end.

3.3.3.1. Corrective actions taken

- The OTP issues was escalated to helpdesk and to IT. Temporary solution was given where service providers (Safaricom and Airtel) were contacted, and they communicated that some of the clients had blocked promotional messages hence were unable to receive the OTPS.
- Escalated to the help desk under Ticket Details; Application | ILS - P4 #15706, pending MIP advise.
- IPRS issue was escalated to the Service Provider and the user passwords were reset.
- Escalated to the help desk and resolved by the MIP team after the new patch was deployed to Live environment.

3.3.4. Potential Risks and Threats

- Sensitivity of the business to internal and external shocks (e.g., agent behaviour, employers' dynamics that may affect collections and disbursements).
- Agent Model instability: agent recruitment/attraction/retention difficulties.

3.3.5. Competitor Activity

- Competition has responded to consumer demands/preferences via loan tenor extensions as well as enhanced agent remuneration offering (9.5% new customer deals and 8% rollovers/top-ups).

3.3.6. New Legislation

- New proposed regulation of Credit only MFIs and Digital lending still in progress.

3.4. Current sales focus areas

- Sales agents hiring distributed in sites with civil service populations
- Sales teams rationalisation for efficiency
- Prospects data activations (we have obtained ~26000 MFI borrowing prospects which the field teams are working on for appointments and closing)

3.5. Collections focus areas

- Follow up on outstanding payments from counties
- Distressed Accounts finalization
- Restatements of NPLs
- Clean-up of provisions through write offs.
- Retrace of accounts
- Deceased accounts finalization

A graphical snapshot of the key results for the month can also be presented as below.

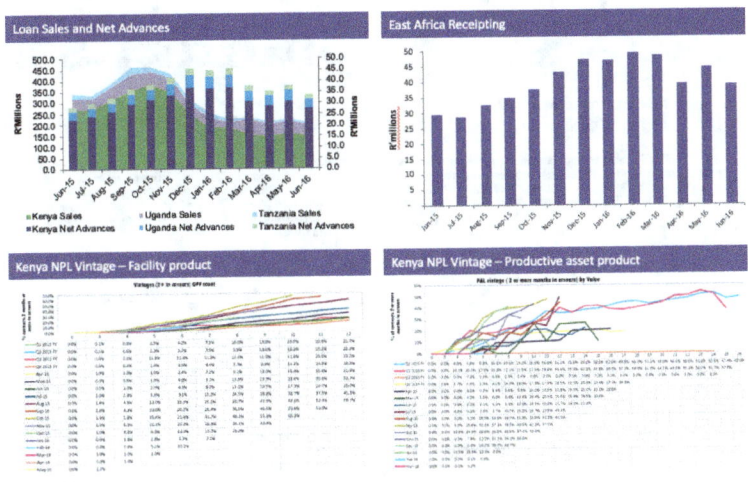

Operating environment report

The environment within which the MFI operates needs to be documented and updated at least monthly, giving attention to the key economic aspects of the political jurisdiction. A sample of such a report is given under.

Your sustainable microfinance business guide

Sample report:

3.1. Country Overview
3.1.1. Outlook

The Central Bank of Kenya (CBK) introduced a Chief Executive Officers' (CEOs) Survey in March 2021, with the objective of capturing information on top firms' perceptions, expectations and decisions and supporting key policy decisions, including monetary policy. The Survey supplements the Monetary Policy Committee (MPC) Private Sector Market Perceptions, and Survey of Hotels. The results of Survey provide valuable input to the Monetary Policy Committee (MPC) at its meetings.

The Survey sought CEOs views on selected indicators including business confidence/optimism, previous quarter business activity, and outlook for business activity in the near term. The survey also sought to establish the key internal and external factors that could influence the business outlook, and strategic priorities over the medium-term. The key expectations on growth prospects from the May 2021 CEOs Survey are summarized in the table below.

The growth prospects over the next 12 months (% of respondents)

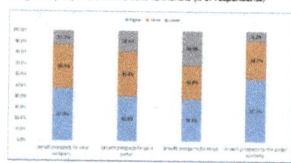

3.1.2. Macroeconomic Indicators
3.1.2.1. Exchange rates

The Kenya Shilling remained stable against major international and regional currencies during the week ending July 1. It exchanged at KSh 107.92 per US dollar on July 1, compared to KSh 107.77 per US dollar on June 24.

3.1.2.2. Foreign Exchange Reserves

The usable foreign exchange reserves remained adequate at USD 9,494 million (5.81 months of import cover vs 4.59 in May-21) as at July 1 (meets the 4 months of import cover, and the EAC region's convergence criteria of 4.5 months of import cover targets).

3.1.2.3. Money Markets

The money market was liquid during the week ending July 1, supported by government payments, which offset tax remittances. Commercial banks' excess reserves remained above the 4.25 % cash reserves requirement (CRR). The average interbank rate was 4.82 % on July 1 compared to 5.00 % on June 24.

3.1.2.4. Inflation rate

Overall inflation edged up but remained within the target range. It increased to 6.3 % in June from 5.9 % in May, mainly on account of higher food and fuel prices.

Trends in broad inflation categories in %

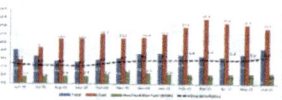

3.1.2.5. Government Securities and Bond Markets

The Treasury bills auction of July 1 was oversubscribed by 30.6 %. Interest rates on the Treasury bills declined. The tap sale of two 20-year Fixed rate Treasury bonds on June 30 that were reopened during the June 16 were undersubscribed by 33.0 %.

Government Securities Yield Curve

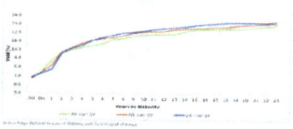

Turnover of bonds traded in the domestic secondary market declined by 38.3 % during the week ending July 1.

3.1.2.6. Equity Market

At the Nairobi Securities Exchange, the NASI and the NSE 20 share price index increased by 1.90 % and 1.94 % respectively, during the week ending July 1(the highest level of NASI since April 5, 2018, and the highest level of the NSE 20 share price index since July 20, 2020). Market capitalisation also increased by 1.9 % during the week. However, equity turnover and total shares traded declined by 26.7 % and 20.9 %, respectively.

3.1.2.7. Credit market overview

Mobile loans
New accounts opened by mobile lenders are steadying. The banking sector leads the market in the number of mobile loan accounts opened, followed by microfinance lenders. Mobile loans still carry more risk than other loan types.

Personal loans
Most personal loans are held by retail market clients and dominated by check-off loans. The emergence of mobile loans and mobile wallets has contributed to greater financial inclusion and reinforced the growth of digitized personal loans.

Asset finance loans
The agricultural, transport and construction sectors have a high demand for asset finance products. The Millennial and Generation X cohorts make up 81% of asset finance loans issued; a factor lender should consider when offering finance for these assets, particularly phones.

Overdraft
Overdraft facilities have gained significant uplift in the market in the last quarter. Facilities extended grew threefold, driven mainly by the banking sector and uptake of Fuliza – a service that allows M-PESA customers to complete their M-PESA transactions when they have insufficient funds in their M-PESA account.

Credit cards
Although the uptake of credit cards in Kenya remains low, the convenience and rewards they offer make them attractive to borrowers. Recent market shifts present several opportunities for lenders to grow their credit card portfolios.

Mortgages
At KES 19.2 million, the average mortgage lending limit is high. Affordable housing projects aimed at the low- and medium-income markets will create significant potential for lenders to grow their mortgage portfolios.

Trade finance loans
Most banks are focusing on trade finance solutions for small and medium-sized enterprises (SMEs). There's a growing emphasis on reducing application approval turnaround times and increasing the use of blockchain technology to facilitate letters of credit and mitigate potential fraud between trading partners.

Summary:

- Total loan accounts increased from 153.4 million in Q4 to 180.6 million in Q1 2021 (+17.7%).
- Overdraft facilities increased by over 12.0 million, from 21.6 million in Q4 2020 to 33.7 million at the end of Q1 2021 (+56.1%).
- Interestingly, mobile loan accounts increased by over 13.8 million, from 103.9 million in Q4 2020 to 117.7 million at the close of Q1 2021.
- This positive credit growth shows a healthy financial system and a stable macroeconomic environment.

Overview of the Kenyan credit market, Q1 2021

Loan type	Market percentage	New market value (KES)		Max loans issued	
Mobile	65.2%	60.28	+2.4%	4.42M	+0.4%
Personal	1.7%	82.98	+24.0%	182.5M	+29.4%
Business	1.7%	152.40	+53.8%	95.3M	+4.2%
Asset Finance	0.2%	13.10	+87.1%	5.7M	+4.9%
Trade Finance	0.2%	92.30	+20.6%	4.3L	+0.9%
Overdraft	18.8%	33.98	+77.6%	10.3M	+42.7%
Credit cards	0.3%	125.2M	+8.3%	4.5M	+17.0%
Mortgages	0.3%	36.7M	+52.7%	1.7K	+17.6%

Looking ahead
Consumer behaviours and the risk landscape have shifted. The sustained financial impact of the COVID-19 crisis is driving lenders to revisit practices for acquiring customers and managing risk. Future-focused lending institutions will speed up their drive to digital transformation to satisfy emerging demands. Future success will require improving customer engagement, increasing operational efficiency, and managing risk in innovative ways. Successful lenders will invest in advanced data analytics for improved marketing and sophisticated digital security to protect customers' data.

Credit Analyses

The critical numbers to monitor from a credit performance analysis in an MFI are presented below.

Loan collection rates

The graphs below show how collections from the various loan performance bands can be presented in a summary format.

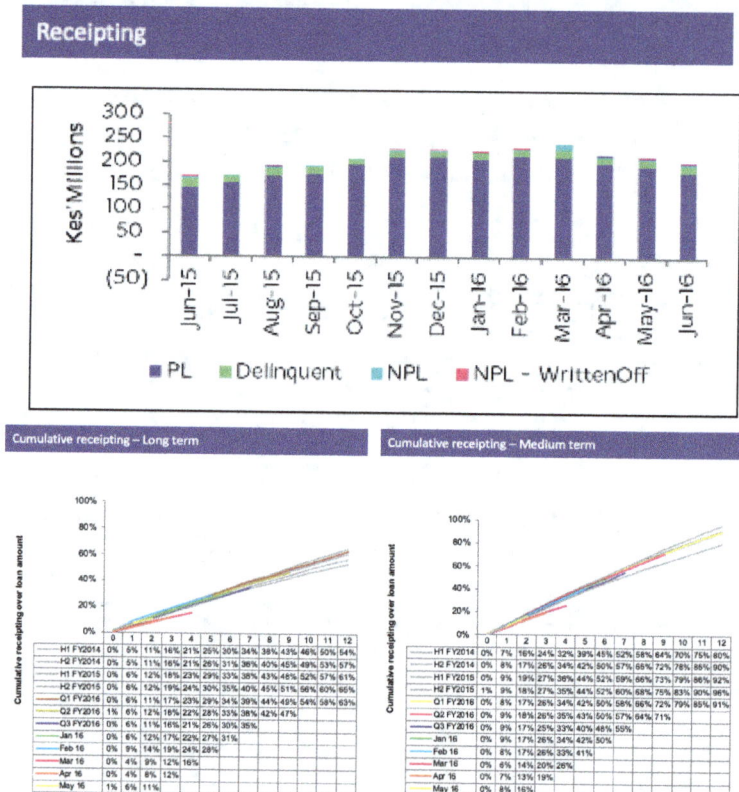

Credit Quality

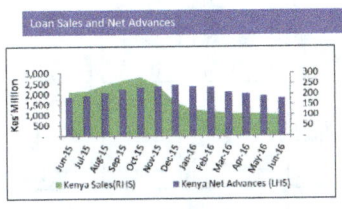
Loan Sales and Net Advances

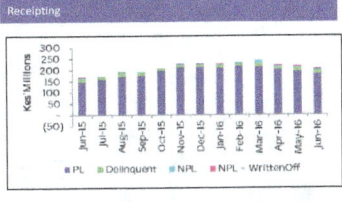
Receipting

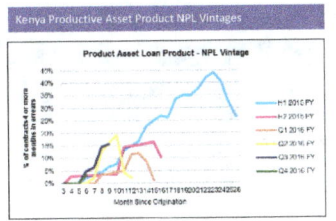
Kenya Productive Asset Product NPL Vintages

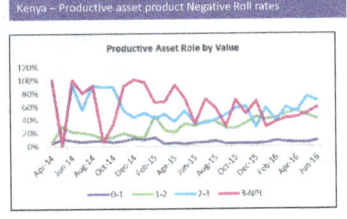
Kenya – Productive asset product Negative Roll rates

Financial Analyses

The Key financial analytics required for an MFI would be presented as snapshots with commentary of each line item as follows:

    i.   Financial statements
          a.   Balance sheet

Balance Sheet

Balance sheet	Apr 2015 Actual Kes'm	May 2015 Actual Kes'm	June 2015 Actual Kes'm	Apr 2016 Actual Kes'm	May 2016 Actual Kes'm	June 2016 Actual Kes'm	Jun 2016 Budget Kes'm	M.o.M Jun/16 Var %	June 2016 Act vs Bud %	Y.o.Y 2016 vs 2015 Var %
Net advances	2,111	2,235	2,205	2,435	2,331	2,215	2,397	-5%	-8%	0%
Other assets	303	311	383	447	458	502	600	10%	-16%	31%
Cash and cash equivalents	295	262	162	530	627	688	117	10%	>100%	>100%
Total assets	2,710	2,808	2,750	3,411	3,416	3,405	3,114	0%	9%	24%
Equity	581	596	643	936	954	817	737	-14%	11%	27%
Bond MTN	-	-	-	1,515	1,537	1,559	1,615	1%	-3%	-
Deferred and current tax liabilities	34	33	57	-89	-80	-72	(19)	-10%	>100%	<100%
Long term debt & accounts payable	2,094	2,179	2,050	1,049	1,005	1,102	781	10%	41%	-46%
Total equity and liabilities	2,710	2,808	2,750	3,411	3,416	3,405	3,114	0%	9%	24%

The above presents the key balance sheet items in a trend format and comparing with the month's budget. The next presentation lays emphasis on the current period's actual results against the period's budget while also presenting the next quarter's budget.

Your sustainable microfinance business guide

Balance sheet

	Mar-16 Actual Kes 'm	Jun-16 Budget Kes 'm	Sep-16 Budget Kes 'm	Dec-16 Budget Kes 'm	Mar-17 Budget Kes 'm	2017 v 2016
Net Loans & Advances	2,539	2,163	2,065	2,088	2,150	-15%
Property & Equipment	115	159	145	130	116	1%
Other assets	573	441	430	420	310	-46%
Cash and cash equivalents	457	404	331	314	23	-95%
Total assets	**3,684**	**3,167**	**2,971**	**2,952**	**2,598**	**-29%**
Tier I Capital	326	222	222	232	251	-23%
Tier I Capital	-	1,329	1,177	1,081	751	
Long term interest bearing loans	3,334	1,615	1,567	1,630	1,581	-53%
Other liabilitites	25	0	5	10	15	-39%
Total equity and liabilities	**3,684**	**3,167**	**2,971**	**2,952**	**2,598**	**-29%**

b. Income statement (Profit or loss statement)

Statement of financial performance

	Month Jun 2015 Kes'm	Month Apr 2016 Kes'm	Month May 2016 Kes'm	Month Jun 2016 Kes'm	Month June Bud Kes'm	YTD Jun-16 Act Kes'm	YTD Jun-16 Bud Kes'm	YTD Jun-15 Act Kes'm	M.o.M Jun 16 Var %	YTD Jun 16 Act vs Bud %	Y.o.Y 2016 vs 2015 Var %
Performing loans net yield	83	56	45	11	34	111	143	240	-76%	-22%	-54%
Interest and fee income	82	104	102	98	81	305	259	247	-4%	18%	23%
Impairment provision	1	(49)	(57)	(87)	(47)	(194)	(116)	(7)	52%	66%	>100%
Non-Performing loans net yield	(10)	11	6	1	3	18	15	(25)	-77%	23%	<100%
Interest and fee income	8	13	11	11	19	35		26	7%		35%
Impairment provision	(20)	(3)	(7)	(14)	(16)	(24)		(53)	>100%	-	-55%
Other interest income	1	1	2	4	0	7	0	2	>100%	-	>100%
Net yield	73	67	50	12	37	129	157	215	-76%	-18%	-40%
Finance costs	(17)	(35)	(34)	(34)	(31)	(103)	(94)	(53)	-2%	9%	94%
Bond interest	0	(22)	(22)	(22)	(22)	(66)	(66)	0	-3%	-1%	-
Intercompany interest	(17)	(13)	(12)	(12)	(9)	(37)	(28)	(53)	-1%	32%	-31%
Net margin	56	32	16	(22)	6	26	63	162	<100%	-58%	-84%
Operating expenditure	(55)	(51)	(50)	(55)	(57)	(156)	(158)	(159)	9%	-1%	-2%
Contribution	1	(19)	(34)	(77)	(51)	(130)	(95)	4	>100%	36%	<100%
Attributable to providers of qualifying tier II capital	(6)	(7)	(7)	(7)	(7)	(20)	(21)	(17)	0%	-4%	14%
Foreign exchange gain (loss)	0	(41)	151	(118)	(31)	(8)	9	(62)	<100%	<100%	-86%
One off restructure costs				(24)	(24)	(24)	(24)			0%	
Attributable to ordinary shareholders	(5)	(67)	110	(225)	(113)	(182)	(130)	(75)	<100%	39%	>100%
Commentary											

Gross Yields
Overall marginal reduction of yields (both PL & NPL) by Kes 4m largely as a result of flat sales and receipting under performance as the divisions overall position this year is to maintain the size of the book with no anticipation on growth of gross yield numbers.

Impairments
Impairment charges were slightly higher in June than in May (both PL & NPL) (by 58%) attributable mainly to the increased negative rolls across most buckets, but mostly in the 3 months in arrears bucket into NPL. Increased rolls from bucket 3 to NPL is as a result of underperformance in receipting. Additional charge of Kes 28M was made to align to the new provision methodology.

Operating Costs
Normal operating costs increased slightly in June 16 as a result of full absorption of retreat costs 4.5M while provision for once off restructure costs scheduled for August 2016 were made in June 2016.

The next presentation is a sample product based profit and loss analysis.

- 59 -

Segmented Contribution Per Product

GPL	Apr-16	May-16	Jun-16	Ytd Jun-16
Gross Yield	76	71	70	216
Impairments	(28)	(42)	(61)	(131)
Net Yield	48	29	9	85
Other income	0	0	0	0
Net operating income	48	29	9	86
Branch staff costs	(3)	(3)	(3)	(9)
Finance costs	(21)	(21)	(21)	(64)
Product contribution	23	5	(15)	13
Other allocated costs				
Admin branch costs	(1)	(1)	(1)	(3)
Head office costs	(7)	(6)	(14)	(27)
Contribution	16	(3)	(30)	(17)
Net Advances	1,380	1,337	1,297	1,297

PAL	Apr-16	May-16	Jun-16	Ytd Jun-16
Gross Yield	25	26	24	75
Impairments	(18)	(19)	(35)	(71)
Net Yield	7	7	(11)	3
Other income	0	0	0	0
Net operating income	7	7	(11)	4
Branch staff costs	(9)	(9)	(9)	(26)
Finance costs	(9)	(9)	(9)	(26)
Product contribution	(10)	(11)	(28)	(49)
Other allocated costs				
Admin branch costs	(2)	(3)	(3)	(8)
Head office costs	(20)	(19)	(40)	(79)
Contribution	(33)	(32)	(71)	(136)
Net Advances	525	493	456	456

Housing	Apr-16	May-16	Jun-16	Ytd Jun-16
Gross Yield	1	1	1	3
Impairments	(0)	(0)	(1)	(2)
Net Yield	1	1	(0)	2
Other income	0	0	0	0
Net operating income	1	1	(0)	2
Branch staff costs	0	0	0	0
Finance costs	(1)	(1)	(1)	(3)
Product contribution	0	(0)	(1)	(2)
Other allocated costs				0
Admin branch costs	(0)	(0)	(0)	(0)
Head office costs	(0)	(0)	(0)	(0)
Contribution	0	(1)	(2)	(2)
Net Advances	64	64	63	63

MEF	Apr-16	May-16	Jun-16	Ytd Jun-16
Gross Yield	0	(0)	0	1
Impairments	0	(0)	0	1
Net Yield	1	(0)	0	1
Other income	0	0	0	0
Net operating income	1	(0)	0	1
Branch staff costs	0	0	0	0
Finance costs	(3)	(3)	(3)	(9)
Product contribution	(2)	(3)	(3)	(8)
Other allocated costs				
Admin branch costs	0	0	0	0
Head office costs	0	0	0	0
Contribution	(2)	(3)	(3)	(8)
Net Advances	12	11	11	11

ii. Financial ratios

Du Pont Analysis

	June 2016 Actual Kes'm	June 2016 Budget Kes'm	June YTD Actual Kes'm	June YTD Budget Kes'm
Average net advances	2,273	2,367	2,327	2,391
Gross yield from assets	59.8%	50.8%	59.6%	43.3%
Lending impairments	-53.5%	-31.8%	-37.4%	-19.5%
Net yield	6.3%	19.0%	22.2%	23.9%
Finance costs	-17.7%	-15.8%	-17.6%	-15.7%
Net margin	-11.5%	3.2%	4.5%	8.1%
Sundry income	0.0%	0.0%	0.0%	0.0%
Net operating income	-11.5%	3.2%	4.5%	8.1%
Operating expenditure	-41.5%	-41.1%	-26.8%	-26.5%
Contribution	-53.0%	-37.9%	-22.3%	-18.4%
Attributable to providers of qualifying tier II capital	-3.5%	-3.6%	-3.4%	-3.4%
Foreign exchange gain (loss)	-62.1%	-15.9%	-1.4%	1.5%
Attributable to ordinary shareholders	-118.5%	-57.5%	-27.2%	-20.3%
Tax	15.9%	11.4%	6.7%	5.5%
ROA	-102.6%	-46.1%	-20.5%	-14.8%
Gearing (Debt/Equity)	2.6	3.0	2.6	3.0
ROE	-263.4%	-137.9%	-52.8%	-44.7%

Key Ratios

KEY RATIO ANALYSIS	MAY 2015	JUN 2015	MAR 2016	APR 2016	MAY 2016	JUN 2016
Monthly Growth Rates						
Total assets	0.3%	-2.3%	-4.3%	-2.7%	0.2%	-0.4%
Total loans and advances	2.7%	0.4%	-11.7%	-2.5%	-4.2%	-5.1%
Total capital employed	10.7%	6.9%	-65.8%	-35.6%	39.8%	-96.5%
Asset Quality						
Credit loss ratio	9.5%	8.8%	19.9%	20.7%	23.4%	29.7%
Open credit exposure ratio	48.3%	60.3%	103.0%	179.4%	136.0%	4027.9%
NPL ratio	14.1%	25.8%	19.3%	21.5%	23.8%	25.0%
Net NPL ratio	5.1%	6.6%	4.0%	4.5%	4.8%	5.1%
Provision coverage - Portfolio	8.4%	4.9%	3.8%	4.0%	4.3%	4.7%
Provision coverage - Specific	53.4%	68.3%	82.2%	81.0%	80.8%	80.7%
W/O assets	88.3%	98.9%	92.0%	91.9%	92.3%	92.3%
Earning Assets/Total Assets	90.7%	89.5%	84.2%	86.8%	86.5%	85.1%
Earnings (Annualised)						
Return on Assets	-5.6%	-5.6%	-6.5%	-17.3%	-3.9%	-17.5%
Return on Equity	-46.3%	-42.3%	-154.7%	-623.4%	-101.0%	-12724.1%
Yield on advances	33.9%	32.8%	34.6%	41.6%	41.8%	41.7%
Fees over interest bearing assets	9.5%	9.4%	7.7%	6.7%	6.2%	6.5%
Cost of debt	7%	7%	12%	15%	15%	14%
Spread	27.3%	26.0%	22.9%	26.8%	27.1%	27.2%
Cost to Income ratio	98.5%	97.1%	61.8%	100.6%	52.8%	83.2%
Staff Costs to Total costs	62.0%	55.1%	59.5%	59.7%	59.4%	64.4%
Staff Costs to Operating Income	61.1%	53.5%	36.8%	60.0%	31.3%	53.6%
Non-Staff costs to Operating income	37.5%	43.6%	25.0%	40.5%	21.4%	29.6%
Non-interest income/net operating income	-23.6%	-7.7%	25.3%	-26.5%	33.6%	12.5%
Liquidity						
Liquid Assets/Total Liabilities	10.7%	6.8%	13.6%	15.9%	19.0%	20.2%

NB: In this computation, Cost to income ratio excludes impairments and the ratio is defined as Operating costs divided by operating income.

iii. Liquidity

Short-term liquidity risk management

A short-term liquidity policy ensures that all cash pay-out obligations over the immediate 12-month period can be met. This is achieved when for the 12-month period the available cash and unused credit facilities are sufficient to meet the net cash outflow of the MFI, where Net cash outflow is defined as 90% of anticipated receipts less all debt repayments and operating expenses. This excludes any payments or cashflows relating to any non-recourse special-purpose funding entities.

Long Term Liquidity Management - Cumulative mismatch limit

In the long-term, 75% of expected cumulative receipting must exceed the cumulative cash outflows relating to debt repayments (capital and interest). This should be measured on a monthly basis and excludes cash flows relating to Non-Recourse Funding SPVs.

Example:

Your sustainable microfinance business guide

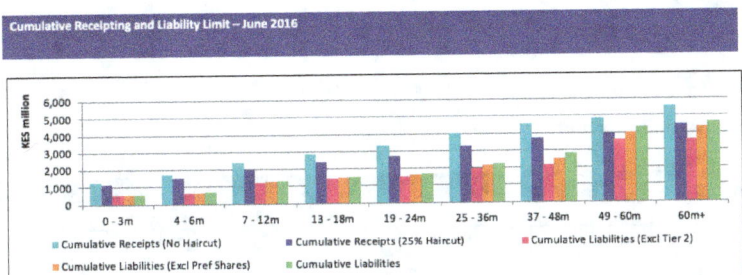

iv. Capital Management

Illustrative

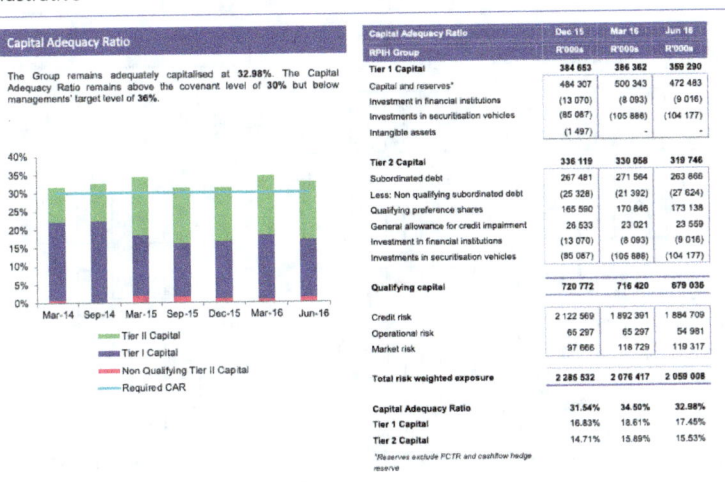

- 62 -

Your sustainable microfinance business guide

Appendix

Loan Application form

PERSONAL DETAILS

Surname: ☐☐☐☐☐☐☐☐☐☐☐☐ First Name(s): ☐☐☐☐☐☐☐☐☐☐

Title: ☐ Mr. ☐ Mrs. ☐ Miss. ☐ Dr. ☐ Prof. Gender: ☐ Male ☐ Female

ID/Passport No: ☐☐☐☐☐☐☐☐☐☐ Date of Birth: ☐☐☐☐☐☐☐☐

Other Names: ☐☐☐☐☐☐☐☐☐☐ Nationality: ☐☐☐☐☐☐☐☐☐☐

Email Address: ☐☐☐☐☐☐☐☐☐☐☐☐☐☐☐☐☐☐☐☐☐☐

CONTACT DETAILS

Home: ☐☐☐☐☐☐☐☐☐☐ Work: ☐☐☐☐☐☐☐☐☐☐ Spouse Mobile: ☐☐☐☐☐☐☐☐☐☐

Mobile: ☐☐☐☐☐☐☐☐☐☐ Work Fax: ☐☐☐☐☐☐☐☐☐☐ Spouse Work: ☐☐☐☐☐☐☐☐☐☐

PHYSICAL ADDRESS

	Home Address	Employment/ Business Address
Block/House No		
Block/ House Name		
Street		
Village/Estate		
Date of Occupation		
Residential Status	☐ Owner ☐ Tenant ☐ Other	☐ Owner ☐ Tenant ☐ Other

POSTAL ADDRESS

Postal Code: ☐☐☐☐☐☐ City/Town: ☐☐☐☐☐☐☐☐

OTHER PARTICULARS

Education Level: ☐ None ☐ Primary ☐ Secondary ☐ College ☐ University

Marital Status: ☐ Married ☐ Divorced ☐ Widowed ☐ Single Number of Dependents: ☐☐☐

NEXT OF KIN

Name: ☐☐☐☐☐☐☐☐☐☐☐☐ Relationship: ☐☐☐☐☐☐☐☐☐☐

ID/Passport No: ☐☐☐☐☐☐☐☐☐☐ Contact No: ☐☐☐☐☐☐☐☐☐☐

PERSONAL CREDIT HISTORY

List all loans held during the last five years.

Lender	Balance Outstanding	Date granted	Term	Monthly Payment	Loan Amount

Have you ever been declined for a loan? ☐ Yes   ☐ No   Details: _____

Do you have any outstanding judgements? ☐ Yes   ☐ No   Details: _____

CONSENT

I consent to the following:

- ☐ Confidential information disclosed in this application may be used to conduct a credit check on me at any registered credit bureau or other registered financial institutions.

- ☐ A copy of my National ID/Passport will be submitted as part of the credit application.

- ☐ The loan officer may take photographs of me as part of the application process.

- ☐ The loan officer may take photographs of my personal residence during the application process.

Date	Applicant(Signature)	Witness(Signature)

Sample Credit underwriting process

General Purpose Facility Business Rules

1	Introduction	
1.1		Business rules will be a set of rules that explain the requirements and the limits that apply to General Purpose Facility. These rules will be in place to ensure that we operate efficiently, promptly, within the legal requirements and achieve company objectives.
2	Entities Business rules	
2.1	Borrower	
2.1.1		The borrower must be a Kenyan Citizen
2.1.2		The borrower must be 18 years old and not older than 65 years
2.1.3		The borrower should not have any criminal records
2.1.3.1		The borrower should have operated the business for a minimum of 2 years in permanent business premises –
2.1.4		The business must be legal
2.2	Guarantor	
2.2.1	Must be provided	
2.2.1.1		Where there is questionable credit history and / or Has been listed in CRB before and is now cleared
2.2.1.2		Those who have not been rated in a CRB report
2.2.1.3		Where adequate security is lacking
2.2.1.4		All clients who provide chattels as security must provide guarantors who will not necessarily provide securities
2.2.2		Security provided by guarantor must be verifiable
2.2.3		Guarantor can provide securities to guarantee up to 25% of the loan where there is inadequate security
2.3	Lending to guarantor:	
2.3.1		Normal business rules apply
2.3.2		Guarantor substitution rules apply where need be
2.3.3		Security used cannot be re-used
2.3.4		System ability to track the guarantee ship and security tracking mechanism is key
2.4		Companies will require personal guarantees from Directors.

Your sustainable microfinance business guide

2.5		The guarantor should complete and sign the guarantor's agreement (Deed of guarantee).
2.6		Referees
2.6.1		1 referee who must be a close relative (must be 18yrs)
2.6.2		The referee and next of kin must be different
3	Borrower Documents	
3.1		Current business permit (current mandatory trading licenses) and proof of existence for the 2 years should be provided
3.2		Proof of existence
3.2.1		Any previous year business permit
3.2.2		Other licenses e.g. health, food, pharmacy, etc annexure on specific special permits.
3.2.3		Lease agreement (current or previous year)
3.2.4		Evidence of payment of rent for previous year
3.3		At least the latest Three month sales records
3.4		Bank statement for latest 3 months
3.5		Current Lease agreement or proof of owner occupier must be adduced. A letter from the landlord will be accepted in absence of a lease agreement.
3.6		Tax registration proof e.g. Personal Identification Number (PIN)
3.7		National identification document e.g. Identification Card (ID), Passport
3.8		Business registration certificate for registered business
3.9		If borrower is a company
3.9.1		Memorandum and articles of Association for companies
3.9.2		Resolution to borrow for companies.
3.9.3		Latest annual returns
3.9.4		Certificate of incorporation
4	Guarantor documents	
4.1.1		National identification document e.g. ID, Passport
4.1.2		Tax registration proof e.g. PIN
4.1.3		Deed of guarantee
4.1.4		Chattel mortgage instrument

5 Facility Documents checks

5.1 National Identity card /Passport

5.1.1 The Loan Officer must certify ID/Passport copy as true copy of the original

5.1.2 ID waiting card or police abstract will not be accepted

5.1.3 Bad image quality (ID number, name not clear) will not be accepted

5.2 PIN certificate

5.2.1 Copy of the PIN certificate

5.3 Bank Statements (latest 3 months)

5.3.1 Latest 90 days bank statement

5.3.2 Bank account details must be for customer

5.3.3 Statement must be stamped and certified as a true copy

5.3.4 Bank statement cannot be older than 10 days from the date of the stamp

5.4 Lease agreement / proof of owner occupier

5.4.1 Lease agreement must be signed by both the borrow and the landlord

5.4.2 A copy of title deed bearing the borrowers details will act as a proof of owner occupier.

5.4.3 In absence of Lease agreement, a letter from the Landlord signed by the Landlord

5.5 Enterprise

5.5.1 Business permits

5.5.1.1 Current business permit (current mandatory trading licenses) and proof of existence for the 2 years should be provided

5.5.1.2 The permits should be printed in stationary bearing the name of the local authority where the business is located.

5.5.1.3 Special permits/Licences for certain business and professions e.g. liquor licence for bars, practising certificate for doctors etc.,

5.5.1.4 Proof of payment for renewal of permit in absence of the current year's business permit

5.5.2 Certificate of business registration if business permit is not in customers name

5.5.2.1		Registration of business names must have the business and customer name
5.5.2.1.1.		In cases that the registration is not in the name of the borrower, proof of ownership must be provided.in form of an affidavit
5.5.2.1.2.		Must be dated and signed by a government official
5.5.2.1.3.		Some businesses are not in the name of owner but are not necessarily registered. For instance we have very many retail shops just in the names of the clients' children or an appealing theme. In such a case we should consider an affidavit or maybe the receipt used to pay for the permits which normally then have the official names. This plus the lease agreement can be used together as proof of ownership.
5.5.3	Memorandum and articles of association for Companies	
5.5.3.1		Certified copies of companies memorandum and Articles of Association and Certificate of Incorporation duly certified by an attorney.
5.5.3.2		The articles of Association should indicate the borrowing power of the directors.
5.5.3.3		The Memorandum and articles of association should be accompanied by a Resolution to borrow prepared by the Directors and sealed with the company seal.
5.5.3.4		Search certificate obtained from registrar of companies.
5.5.4	Sales records	
5.5.4.1		Latest 3 consecutive months sales records
5.5.4.2		In the event of businesses that are highly sensitive to seasons, high, medium and low seasons sales will be considered for the last one year period.
5.6	Credit Reference Bureau Report	
5.6.1		Should be in credit reference bureau letter head
5.6.2		Should not be more 10 days old.
5.6.3		Personal information on the report should match the customer details
5.6.4		The report should have a credit score summary for individual and companies
5.6.4.1		Where the company has a Nil score the directors score to be used

5.6.5		The report should have detailed credit performance data.
5.6.6		The details on the report should be clear.
5.7	Securities and guarantee	
5.7.1	Land title deed	
5.7.1.1		Title details must bear customer's/guarantor's name
5.7.1.2		All other land details e.g. title deed number, land size etc should be clear
5.7.1.3		Should be free from any encumbrances
5.7.1.4		Land title deed should be accompanied by the following before initiating the perfection process;
5.7.1.4.1.		Official search from the Land Registry
5.7.1.4.2.		Valuation report from an appointed Valuer
5.7.1.5		Land title deed should be accompanied by the following before disbursement;
5.7.1.5.1.		Registered charge document stamped at the Lands registry.
5.7.2	Motor Vehicle Log Book	
5.7.2.1		The log book should be in the name of the borrower or the guarantor.
5.7.2.2		The log book details should be clear and they should match with the car details.
5.7.2.3		The log book should be accompanied by the following before perfection process starts;
5.7.2.3.1.		Search from Kenya revenue authority
5.7.2.3.2.		Valuation report from an appointed evaluator
5.7.2.4		The log book should accompanied by a duly filled and signed transfer form, official search from Kenya Revenue authority (KRA),copy of National Identity card or passport the borrower/guarantor or a Certificate of Business Registration in the case of corporate bodies and the pin card of the borrower/guarantor before disbursement.
5.7.2.5		The signature on the log book should match the signature in the transfer form.
5.7.3	Chattels Mortgage instrument	

5.7.3.1		Chattels Mortgage instrument must be drawn up and executed by an attorney.
5.7.3.2		Chattels Mortgage instrument must be registered and stamped by Registrar of Companies. This can be done after approval by the credit dept i.e security perfection as the branches do not have this capacity currently.
5.7.4		Guarantor Deed of Guarantee and Indemnity
5.7.4.1		The guarantee should be a continues guarantee to cover the facility term
5.7.4.2		The Deed of Guarantee and Indemnity should include the following provisions:
5.7.4.2.1.		Definitions and Interpretation
5.7.4.2.2.		Guarantee and Indemnity
5.7.4.2.3.		Demand on Guarantors
5.7.4.2.4.		Guarantee not affected by various matters
5.7.4.2.5.		Guarantors Warranties and Declarations
5.7.4.2.6.		Trust Provisions
5.7.4.2.7.		Notices
5.7.4.2.8.		Execution under Power of Attorney
5.7.4.2.9.		Signing by the Borrower
5.7.4.2.10.		Governing Law
5.7.4.2.11.		Independent Legal Advice
5.7.4.2.12.		Joint and Several Liability
6	Process Flow business rules	
6.1	Pre-validation	
6.1.1		To be done at the customer's business site
6.1.2		Loan officer will look at the following documents
6.1.2.1		New customers;
6.1.2.1.1.		Current Business permits
6.1.2.1.2.		At least the latest three month sales records
6.1.2.1.3.		Lease agreement or proof of owner occupier
6.1.2.1.4.		Tax registration proof e.g. PIN

6.1.2.1.5.		National identification document e.g. ID, passport
6.1.2.1.6.		Business registration certificate for registered business
6.1.2.1.7.		Memorandum and articles of Association for companies
6.1.2.1.8.		The latest three months certified bank statement
6.1.2.2		Facility renew
6.1.2.2.1.		Facility will be renewed every 12monthsCustomer initiated facility review capped to 6 months from the initial facility review
6.1.2.2.2.		Document requirements
6.1.2.2.2.1.		Current business permits
6.1.2.2.2.2.		At least the latest three month sales records
6.1.2.2.2.3.		Lease agreement or proof of owner occupier
6.1.2.2.2.4.		The latest three months certified bank statement-removed
6.1.2.2.2.5.		CRB report
6.1.3		Loan Officer will use the last three months sales estimates to determine if the customer will qualify for a new facility.
6.1.4		The Loan officer will also factor other borrowings that the customer has to determine the maximum instalment amount.
6.1.5		Loan Officer issues the customer with facility offer if pre-validation indicates that the customer will qualify for the facility
6.1.5.1		If the customer has paid the previous limit well and due to system factors the client cannot qualify for the said limit, then maintain the previous limit.
6.1.6		The customer should accept the offer within 30days.
6.2	Affordability	
6.2.1		Main business income plus other business incomes
6.2.1.1		Field-level verification
6.2.1.1.1.		The Loan officer must confirm the facility applicant's business activities and collect as much ground level information as necessary to enable prudent credit decision
6.2.1.1.2.		For new customers, in instances where a facility applicant does not maintain complete and reliable books of accounts, financial data for the affordability calculations will be estimated from proxies such as bills/confirmation from suppliers, physical stock verification etc.

6.2.1.1.3.	The Loan officer should verify accuracy of information on the business situation and prospects provided by the client through other sources like customers, employees, suppliers and competitors, and his or her own understanding of the market and the dynamics of the client's type of business built over time.
6.2.1.2	Calculation of Maximum facility Size
6.2.1.2.1.	The maximum facility size available to a customer is derived from the size of the businesses and the ability of the borrower to repay the loan.
6.2.1.2.2.	Basic principles:
6.2.1.2.2.1.	The customer should be able to repay the loan from the cash flow generated from use of the loan in the business. This will ensure that the business is able to meet the loan obligations. If the cash flow generated from use of the loan is smaller than the loan instalments, the loan will burden the business and should not be granted.
6.2.1.2.2.2.	The cash flow from the use of the facility should always be identified and compared to the loan instalment.
6.2.1.2.2.2.1.	30% of average monthly sales to be reflected in the bank statement of loans above 1M.
6.2.1.2.2.3.	The facility must result in profits for the business to be beneficial rather than a burden to the business.
6.2.1.3	Maximum facility instalment
6.2.1.3.1.	Based on business type, maximum instalment equals lessor of
6.2.1.3.1.1.	10 % of sales
6.2.1.3.1.2.	20% of gross profit
6.2.1.3.1.2.1.	Plus affordability from additional incomes
6.2.1.3.1.3.	Reduced by existing debt instalments
6.2.1.4	Where clients don't have structured sales records then;
6.2.1.4.1.	Client to have 100% of the instalment less other borrowings, reflected in the bank statement month on month (6 months statement)
6.2.1.4.2.	Seasonality of the business will be considered
6.2.1.5	Minimum monthly instalment

6.2.1.5.1.	Instalment calculated by re amortizing the loan over minimum amortization period (currently 12 months) subject to:
6.2.1.5.1.1.	Minimum repayment of Kes10,000 or
6.2.1.5.1.2.	Current balance if less than the Minimum Instalment
6.2.1.5.2.	Instalment to remain unchanged if no disbursement during the month
6.2.1.5.3.	Instalment to be re-calculated if interest rate changes
6.2.1.6	Character assessment
6.2.1.6.1.	The customer should provide the Loan Officer with details of at least three references, two of who know and do business with the applicant and one who is a relative.
6.2.1.6.2.	If the customer has borrowed from Real People before, it is essential to check whether the loan was repaid as agreed.
6.2.1.6.3.	Sources of information for a character reference:
6.2.1.6.3.1.	Customers
6.2.1.6.3.2.	Suppliers
6.2.1.6.3.3.	Employees
6.2.1.6.3.4.	Neighbours
6.2.1.6.3.5.	Banks
6.2.1.6.3.6.	Close relatives
6.2.1.6.3.7.	Community/church leaders
6.2.1.6.3.8.	Documentation e.g. bank statements
6.2.1.6.3.9.	Site visit
6.2.1.7	Affordability documents;
6.2.1.7.1.	At least the latest three month sales records
6.2.1.7.2.	Bank statement for latest 3 months
6.2.1.7.3.	Rent receipts where applicable for rental houses.
6.2.2	Guarantor assessment
6.2.2.1	Guarantors should be interviewed.
6.2.2.2	The borrow should identify the guarantor
6.2.2.3	The guarantor should complete and sign the guarantor's agreement (Deed of guarantee).

6.2.2.4		Loan Officer should verify if the guarantor is guaranteeing any other loans.
6.2.3	Facility renew	
6.2.3.1		The Loan Officer should call or visit the previous guarantor(s) to ascertain if s/he is still willing to guarantee the client's next facility.
6.2.3.2		If the client has a new guarantor, s/he should be interviewed using the same set of questions for guarantors in the initial process.
6.2.4	Loan officer will look at the following documents;	
6.2.4.1		National identification document e.g. ID, passport
6.2.4.2		Tax registration proof e.g. PIN
6.2.5	Credit Reference Bureau	
6.2.5.1		Loan officer should send customer name and National ID to Head office Vetting department
6.2.5.2		The vetting department should get the customer's Credit Bureau Report using the customer details and forward the same to the loan officer.
6.2.5.3		Only customer with positive credit rating will have their loan approved.
6.3	Centralised Vetting	
6.3.1	Document vetting	
6.3.1.1		Borrowers Documents vetting
6.3.1.1.1.		Business permits for current and proof of existence for the last two years
6.3.1.1.2.		Lease agreement /proof of owner occupier/ Landlord letter
6.3.1.1.3.		Rent receipts where applicable
6.3.1.1.4.		Tax registration proof e.g. PIN
6.3.1.1.5.		National identification document e.g. ID, passport
6.3.1.1.6.		Business registration certificate for registered business
6.3.1.1.7.		Memorandum and articles of Association for companies
6.3.1.1.8.		Resolution to borrow for companies sealed with the company seal
6.3.1.1.9.		Latest Annual returns for companies

6.3.1.1.10.	Certificate of incorporation for companies
6.3.1.1.11.	Credit Bureau Report
6.3.1.2	Guarantor
6.3.1.2.1.	National identification document e.g. ID, passport
6.3.1.2.2.	Signed and executed Deed of guarantee form
6.3.1.3	Affordability Vetting
6.3.1.3.1.	A sample of the latest sales records
6.3.1.3.2.	Certified Bank statement for latest 3 months not older than 10 days
6.3.1.3.3.	Vetting clerks checks whether the affordability figures match with sample business records.
6.3.1.4	Referees
6.3.1.4.1.	Vetting clerk to call the referee in order to confirm customer details
6.3.1.5	Securities documents vetting
6.3.1.5.1.	Chattel
6.3.1.5.1.1.	Executed Chattels Mortgage instrument
6.3.1.5.2.	Motor Vehicle
6.3.1.5.2.1.	Search Certificate
6.3.1.5.2.2.	Valuation report
6.3.1.5.2.3.	A duly filled and signed motor vehicle transfer form
6.3.1.5.2.4.	The log Book
6.3.1.5.2.5.	Copies of National Identity card or passport of the borrower/owner or a Certificate of Business Registration in the case of corporate bodies
6.3.1.5.2.6.	Copy of Pin card of the borrower
6.3.1.5.2.7.	Valid comprehensive insurance cover
6.3.1.5.3.	Land
6.3.1.5.3.1.	Valuation report from an appointed evaluator
6.3.1.5.3.2.	Executed Charge document
6.3.1.5.3.3.	Land title deed

6.3.1.6		The customer will sign the Loan agreement once the loan is approved after vetting.
6.3.2	Disbursements	
6.3.2.1		Where land is used as security, disbursement shall only be authorised once an email from the advocate is received stating that the security documents have been successfully lodged in the lands and company registry
6.3.2.2		Where logbook is used as security, disbursement shall only be authorised once legal/vetting confirms the following documents
6.3.2.2.1.		Signed Transfer forms
6.3.2.2.2.		Original Logbook
6.3.2.2.3.		Well executed chattel's form
6.3.2.2.4.		Advance payment by customer
6.3.2.3		Money to be paid to the customer's nominated account
6.3.2.4		Finance department will look at fully signed Drawdown Agreement
7	Draw down	
7.1		Disbursements to be made at request of customer
7.2		Disbursements only paid into customer's nominated account
7.3		Disbursements allowed if
7.3.1		Nil arrears
7.3.2		The facility account is active
7.3.3		The customer has never missed an instalment
7.4		Disbursement amounts
7.4.1		Customer initiated subject to a maximum draw down amount calculated as follows;
7.4.1.1		Facility amount
7.4.1.2		less Current balance
7.5		Subsequent drawdowns pegged to 6months from the initial drawdown
8	Securities	
8.1		Acceptable securities
8.1.1		Primary Securities

8.1.1.1		Chattels over:
8.1.1.1.1.		Business and Household assets
8.1.1.1.2.		Machinery/Equipment
8.1.1.2		Joint Registration over Motor Vehicles
8.1.1.3		Share(Registered by CMA) tied to Lien
8.1.1.4		Debentures(All forms of Debentures)
8.1.1.5		Legal Charge over Land/ Real Estate
8.1.2	Secondary Security	
8.1.2.2		Security based Personal Guarantees
8.1.2.3		Supplementary Debentures (All forms of Debenture under the Companies Act)
8.2	Security Perfection procedure	
8.2.1	Chattels Mortgage	
8.2.1.1		Documentation
8.2.1.1.1.		Perfection of documents prior to registration to take a maximum of 5 days.
8.2.1.1.2.		Chattels Documents must be prepared by external lawyers.
8.2.1.1.2.1.		Cost of documents depends on the scale of fees set out in the Advocates (Remuneration Amendment) Order, 2009.
8.2.1.1.2.2.		Amount payable depends on the value of the transaction.
8.2.1.2		Stamp duty (Stamping)
8.2.1.2.1.		The documents are stamped for a fee
8.2.1.2.2.		The process will take maximum 4 working days.
8.2.1.2.3.		Stamping done at the Land Office.
8.2.1.3		Filing/Registration
8.2.1.3.1.		Documents are filed at the Companies Registry
8.2.1.3.2.		The process will take 1 working day.
8.2.1.4		Under the Chattels Transfer Act, the security instrument itself is registered, instead of the assets encumbered, and the chattels mortgage has to be refreshed every five years.
8.2.1.5		The Chattels Registry requires registration of a chattel's instrument within 21 days of execution.

8.2.2		Motor Vehicle
8.2.2.1		Following are the requirements for transfer of ownership of motor vehicles and trailers to the joint names of Real People and the borrower:
8.2.2.1.1.		A duly filled and signed transfer from "C" obtained from the Road Transport offices in Times Tower, Nairobi, Customs House, Mombasa or the District Commissioners office.
8.2.2.1.2.		The logbook: one is expected to fill up the first vacant 'change' giving his/her full name, address and signature.
8.2.2.1.3.		Copies of National Identity card or passport of both the borrower and the Real People or a Certificate of Business Registration in the case of corporate bodies.
8.2.2.1.4.		Valid insurance cover.
8.2.2.1.5.		Both purchase tax and transfer fee in accordance with the engine capacity rating of the vehicle.
8.2.2.1.6.		Pin cards of both the borrower and Real People.
8.2.3		Land title deed
8.2.3.1		Search of title at the Land Registry
8.2.3.1.1.		Searches at the relevant Land Registry can be carried out by an appointed external party (physical inspection).
8.2.3.1.2.		Requires the physical presence of the person carrying out the search. The Registry in which to conduct the search will depend on the law governing the specific land and where the title is held.
8.2.3.1.3.		Search certificate is issued by the Land Registrar. This is conclusive and the government guarantees title.
8.2.3.1.4.		On average this process takes about 1 working day. However, if the file or title is misplaced or not available, it may take an indeterminate amount of time.
8.2.3.2		Valuation
8.2.3.2.1.		In addition, the borrower must present a valuation report prepared by Real People appointed valuer. This report will also include a valuer's search on the title to the property.
8.2.3.3		Documentation prepared by an appointed attorney
8.2.3.3.1.		Perfection of documents prior to registration will take maximum 5 days.

8.2.3.3.2.	Documents must be prepared by external lawyers.
8.2.3.3.2.1.	Cost of documents depends on the scale of fees set out in the Advocates (Remuneration Amendment) Order, 2009.
8.2.3.3.2.2.	Amount payable depends on the value of the transaction
8.2.3.3.3.	To facilitate registration of the transfer or encumbrance, the following complete documents are required:
8.2.3.3.3.1.	Proof of current land rent and rates
8.2.3.3.3.1.1.	Rates clearance certificate
8.2.3.3.3.1.1.	Issued by the Local Authorities upon payment of a fee.
8.2.3.3.3.1.2.	Valid for 30 days.
8.2.3.3.3.1.3.	Customer need to physically visit the Municipal Council (with supporting documents) to prove that rates have been paid to them before the certificate is issued.
8.2.3.3.3.1.4.	Process needs to be pushed along by the customer or it will not be completed.
8.2.3.3.3.1.5.	Land rent clearance certificate
8.2.3.3.3.1.6.	Issued by the Land Registry upon payment of a fee.
8.2.3.3.3.1.7.	Customer need to physically visit the Registry (with supporting documents) to prove that rent has been paid and to see through the process.
8.2.3.3.3.1.8.	Takes about 14 working days if the correspondence file relating to the property is available; if missing the period is indeterminate.
8.2.3.3.3.1.9.	Four officials within the Land Registry must sign off; delays can occur if these persons are not available.
8.2.3.3.4.	Consent of the Commissioner of Lands
8.2.3.3.4.1.	Required if land is leasehold.
8.2.3.3.5.	Land control board consent
8.2.3.3.5.1.	Required where the land in question is agricultural. Imposed by the Land Control Act. The Land Control Board

		meets once a month in the relevant District to approve the consent at a cost.
8.2.3.3.5.2.		Requires the physical presence of the person requiring the consent.
8.2.3.4		Stamp duty (Stamping)
8.2.3.4.1.		The payment process takes 6 days and involves the assessment, issue of an instrument number against which to make payment at a bank, and subsequent confirmation by the Kenya Revenue Authority to the Land Registry that the stamp duty has been paid, upon which the stamped documents are released to the presenter.
8.2.3.5		Filing/Registration
8.2.3.5.1.		Registration of the security instrument takes place at the Land Office. The exercise takes 7 working days assuming the counterpart title (which is kept at the Land Office) is available as well as the relevant deed file relating to the title. If unavailable the process will take significantly longer.
8.2.3.5.2.		The application for registration has to be accompanied by the original document of title, charge documents, rates clearance certificates, rent clearance certificate, consent and valuation for stamp duty. Except for the Rates Clearance Certificate (Municipal Council) the other documents must have been previously obtained from the Land Registry itself.
8.2.3.5.3.		If the property is owned by a company the particulars of the instrument constituted as collateral have to be filed with the Companies Registry within 42 days of the date of the instrument. The Companies Registry issues a Certificate of Registration.
9		Prohibited business or activities:
9.1		Unregistered traditional herbalist
9.2		Witchdoctors
9.3		Trusts, clubs, NGOs, Churches and ministries
9.4		Any activities involving:-
9.4.1		Forced labour (incl. any involuntary labour extracted under threat of forces.) or
9.4.2		Child labour (incl. the hiring of any person under the age of 18 years).

9.4.3		Production or trade in any product or activity deemed illegal under host country laws or regulation or international conventions and agreements
9.4.4		Any business relating to pornography or prostitution
9.4.5		Trade in wildlife or wildlife products regulated under CITES
9.4.6		Production or use of or trade in hazardous materials such as radioactive materials, unbounded asbestos fibres and products containing PCBs.
9.4.7		Cross-border trade in waste and waste products unless compliant to the Basel Convention and the underlying regulations
9.4.8		Drift net fishing in the marine environment using nets in excess of 2.5 km in length.
9.4.9		Production, use of or trade in pharmaceuticals, pesticides/herbicides, chemicals, ozone depleting substances and other hazardous substances subject to international phase-outs or bans
9.4.10		Destruction of Critical Habitat
9.4.11		Production and distribution of racist, anti-democratic and/or neo-Nazi media.
9.4.12		Commercial logging operations or the purchase of logging equipment for the use in primary tropical moist forest
9.4.13		Production or trade in wood or other forestry products from unmanaged forests
9.4.14		Production or trade in –
9.4.14.1		Weapons and munitions
9.4.14.2		Gambling, casinos and equivalent enterprises
9.4.14.3		Alcoholic beverages.
9.4.14.4		Tobacco

10   Annexure Special permits requirements

No.	Type of Industry	Special licenses/Requirements
	Agrovets	<ul><li>Kenya health inspectorate certificate</li><li>Pest control board license</li><li>Vet professional license for those practicing</li><li>For those selling seeds -seed sellers license</li></ul>
	Bars	<ul><li>liquor license</li><li>food and hygiene licenses (if it's a bar and restaurant)</li></ul>

Business	Licenses
Restaurants/cafes	• Food and hygiene licenses
Chemists/pharmacies	• certificate from the pharmacy and poisons act board (for the individual and for the premise) • certificate of registration for the business
Private Laboratories	• Private medical laboratory practicing licenses, • medical laboratory technologist certificate
Law firms/advocates	• Practicing licenses from the respective bodies
Petrol stations	• NEMA License • fire prevention licenses
Milk supply/retail	• Food and hygiene licenses • Kenya dairy board carriage of milk regulations permits (for those that do supply of the same.
Productions, selling of cds and dvds and showing films	• music copyright license • films classification board license
Private schools	• Certificate of registration from ministry of Education • Certificate of registration from registrar of companies to enable identify the business owners.
surveyors	• Kenya surveyors board licenses
Bakeries	• KEBS license • Food and hygiene
Dental Clinics	• Medical practitioners and Dentist board license for the individual and premise • Certificate of registration for the business
Private Medical hospitals/ Clinics	• Certificate of registration for the medical premise, • Practitioner's license (doctor/nurse) • Certificate of registration from registrar of companies (to ascertain the ownership)
Retail shops that sell gas cylinders and cylinder with gas	• Fire prevention licenses.

Your sustainable microfinance business guide

THIS IS A BLANK PAGE – Final Page

www.ingramcontent.com/pod-product-compliance
Lightning Source LLC
Chambersburg PA
CBHW070258220526
45465CB00004B/1654